"Their Distress is almost intolerable"

The Elias Boudinot Letterbook

1777-1778

Joseph Lee Boyle

HERITAGE BOOKS
2008

HERITAGE BOOKS

AN IMPRINT OF HERITAGE BOOKS, INC.

Books, CDs, and more—Worldwide

For our listing of thousands of titles see our website
at
www.HeritageBooks.com

Published 2008 by
HERITAGE BOOKS, INC.
Publishing Division
100 Railroad Ave. #104
Westminster, Maryland 21157

International Standard Book Number: 978-0-7884-2210-2

CONTENTS

INTRODUCTION

This publication presents the 1777-1778 Elias Boudinot Letterbook and represents his work while serving as Commissary General of Prisoners for the American government. The original manuscript of 152 pages is at the State Historical Society of Wisconsin at Madison. The Society's permission to publish this manuscript is most deeply appreciated.

Boudinot was born in 1740 and died in 1821. He was a prominent attorney in New Jersey at the outbreak of the American Revolution. A member of the New Jersey Assembly, he initially believed that "firm dependence in the mother country essential." But when the Continental Congress declared independence he fully supported the measure.

The Continental Congress had authorized George Washington to appoint a Commissary General of Prisoners, and Washington offered the position to Boudinot on April 1, 1777. Though reluctant to take the assignment he did accept, and wrote his wife he was drawn into "the boisterous noisy, fatiguing unnatural and disrelishing state of War and slaughter" in order to "be of some service to the Prisoners" and "to watch the Military and to preserve the Civil Rights of my Fellow Citizens."

He was elected to the Continental Congress in November 1777, but did not attend until July 1778, largely due to his duties as Commissary General of Prisoners, which he continued to execute until June 1778. He remained in Congress until 1784 and was elected President of that body on November 4, 1782. In this capacity he signed the peace treaty with Great Britain and the treaty of alliance with France, as well as various proclamations ending hostilities and of thanksgiving for the return of peace. He presided at the session when Washington was thanked for his services "in establishing the freedom and independence of your country."

Under the Constitution, which he helped ratify in New Jersey, Boudinot served in Congress 1789-1795, until he became Director of the U.S. Mint in 1795. He served in that capacity until 1805. A wealthy man from his legal work, he retired to study biblical literature and published several religious works himself. He is buried in Burlington, New Jersey. Several biographies are in the list that begins on page 134.

The American colonists took their first enemy prisoners in April 1775, but the Continental Congress did not create a central position for prisoner care until late 1776. This was apparently due to the fact that the number of prisoners held by the Americans was not great, and they were scattered around at various towns in different states. Persons were appointed by the states to look after prisoners, but even after Congress appointed Boudinot, both he and his successors had to contend with reluctance of the states to give up their authority to a central authority.

Congress authorized Washington to appoint a Commissary General of Prisoners, but it was a difficult position to fill. The general offered the job to Boudinot on April 1, 1777, and Boudinot accepted. However Congress had done little more than establish the position, and had failed to define the chain of command, authority, accountability or responsibilities for the position.

Boudinot faced the task of bringing structure to confusion which existed with respect to prisoners of war. Initially with no assistants he was expected to keep accurate records of all prisoners of war, their locations, their expenses and arrange exchanges. As his term progressed he was allowed to appoint a number of assistants at places where significant numbers of prisoners were held, and for specific states. Though his appointment was for all of the thirteen United States, there is no indication he provided any direction or oversight to the Carolinas or Georgia.

To complicate matters Congress had authorized the states to appoint their own commissaries of prisoners. Some states did, others such as Pennsylvania, did not. As will appear by several of the letters that follow, such as that to Abraham Bancker, problems arose as to who was in charge of prisoners in a given geographical area. After Boudinot protested to Congress, that body did not abolish the state systems but decided the state officials were "obliged" to turn over prisoners to Boudinot at his request.

Boudinot was also hampered by the Board of War. Initially composed of members of Congress, then by other appointees, this entity was formed to direct the military effort. But Boudinot felt the Board either did not or would not act on prisoner management matters. In June 1777, Boudinot had discussed the construction of barracks to hold prisoners. In October and December 1777, Boudinot was ordered to have barracks constructed at several locations. The states were to handle construction, but Boudinot was given no funds to pay for construction, nor authority to order the states to do the work.

Throughout the war, Congress issued innumerable, contradictory policy directives on prisoners of war, and every other war related issue. Though wasteful in retrospect, it must be remembered that these men were inventing a government and its operations as they went along, working with slender resources and abysmal communications, while fighting the strongest military power in Europe, and sometimes contending with thirteen state governments whose leaders had their own priorities.

Another problem was that the British did not consider conventional European rules on prisoners of war to apply, as the colonists were considered insurrectionists, not a sovereign nation. The British position was that a formal agreement to exchange prisoners could be viewed as a tacit recognition of American independence, and encourage other countries to recognize the rebels as a country.

Due to these political obstacles, the contending commanders in America engaged in various "partial exchanges." These were simple prisoner trades and had to be individually negotiated as gentlemen's agreements between the generals on their honor. Through this device the British were able to deny they had recognized American sovereignty, thus gaining both their political and military ends.

British reluctance to negotiate exchanges was probably increased by the fact that they took thousands of Americans prisoner in 1776, and held far more captives than the Americans had British or Hessians. The balance switched after John Burgoyne's army surrendered at Saratoga on October 17, 1777.

As will appear by the letters and references to officers who were prisoners, they were not usually kept in close confinement by either side. An officer was considered an honorable man whose word was his bond. Once he had given his word that he would not try to escape, he was usually allowed the freedom of the town he was being held at and a limited area around it. A prisoner officer might get a "parole" which meant he could go back to his side of the lines, but had to remain a non-combatant for an indefinite time until he was "exchanged." Soldiers were usually exchanged for men of the same rank, although scales were developed to show how many privates an officer of a given rank was worth.

Exchanges usually took place with the "oldest" of a given rank being the first exchanged, oldest simply being the longest in captivity. This simple equation was sometimes ignored by the various states who held enemy prisoners, and wanted their own people back, regardless of the preferred protocol. A prime example of this is Boudinot's letter of March 28 to his assistant Ezekiel Williams in Connecticut. Boudinot complains violations of the seniority rules in exchange had a great "Tendency to raise Jealousies & Animosities, between the Troops of the diff. States— This is the reason, the Enemy are so fond of promoting it, by encouraging of these Exchanges—"

As Boudinot's letters show, his problems with prisoner management included trying to feed and clothe our men held by the British, initially in New York, and after September 1777 in Philadelphia. Unlike current protocols, which require the side holding prisoners to provide a certain standard of care, during the Revolutionary War each side was to provide food, clothing, and other aid to its men held by their adversary. This procedure contributed to problems with feeding and clothing the men with the Continental Army at Valley Forge. The men trying to purchase for the active duty soldiers were in competition with Boudinot, who was trying to supply Americans who were prisoners with the enemy, thus helping to raise prices and create shortages. Boudinot was allowed to have agents in Philadelphia and New York, who were to look after the welfare of American prisoners and see that the food and clothing sent in was adequately distributed. However their effectiveness seems to have been limited by British restrictions.

Both Congress and Washington had been concerned throughout 1777 about reports of poor treatment received by American prisoners in New York. Washington had an extensive correspondence with the British commander, Sir William Howe, in an attempt improve conditions. After the enemy captured Philadelphia in September 1777, hundreds of Americans captured during the campaign were held there. Reports of abuse in that city prompted an enquiry by Congress and the Board of War. Howe eventually agreed to allow a "suitable person" to go into

Philadelphia to inspect conditions there. However after Henry Hugh Fergusson, the British Commissary of Prisoners, and Boudinot met in December 1777, Howe would not permit Boudinot into the city. He was not allowed in by the British until June 1778, after Howe had left the command.

In the meantime Boudinot requested permission from Sir Henry Clinton in New York to visit the American prisoners there. This request was granted and Boudinot proceeded to that city and stayed there from February 3-17, 1778. This effort seemed to clear the air and allowed for the improvement of prison conditions. Of course enemy concern over the treatment of the thousands of British and Hessians captured during the Saratoga Campaign is likely to have been a motivating factor. To Boudinot's credit he seemed to have been sincerely concerned that prisoners from both sides of the conflict received satisfactory treatment.

While Boudinot was absent, Washington received a proposal from Howe on February 10, to implement a man for man prisoner exchange. Washington, who was more interested in freeing Americans than the Continental Congress agreed in principle. In August 1777, Congress had authorized him to arrange exchanges whenever and on whatever terms he thought expedient. But on December 19, 1777, Congress had adopted a resolution with outrageous terms for an exchange. One of these was that Congress expected the British to pay in gold or silver for the upkeep of their prisoners held by the Americans, but Congress intended to use its paper money to pay the accounts for Americans held by the British. A few days later Congress resolved that captured Tories be put in jail and sent to their home states for criminal prosecution. Both these conditions were completely unacceptable to the British.

On February 28 Congress reminded Washington of the December resolves to his embarrassment, as the Commander in Chief had already arranged a conference with Howe's deputies to take place on March 10. He then had to ask Howe to postpone the meeting until the end of March. Washington believed that Congressional action curtailed his right to properly negotiate for the exchange of his men. Boudinot wrote that Washington "said his troops looked up to him as their Protector and that he would not suffer an opportunity to be lost in liberating every Soldier who was then in captivity let the Consequence be what it might." Washington was interested in the welfare of his men, but Congress was looking for bigger game—the tacit recognition by the British that America was an independent country, but that recognition was not to be gained through using prisoners as bargaining chips.

After an exchange of correspondence, Congress authorized Washington to negotiate a general cartel for prisoner exchange, but only as "agreeable to the aforementioned resolutions." This effectively meant no general exchange could be acceptable to the British, but Congress did agree that the settlement of the financial accounts did not have to take place before the exchange. Removal of this block allowed some progress to be made.

After the close of this letterbook Boudinot was involved in two conferences for "general cartel" to exchange all prisoners of war. These took place on March 31-April 1 and April 6-11 at Germantown and Newtown, Pennsylvania, respectively. They were not successful as the British would not say anything that would effectively recognize the United States as a independent entity and Congress doggedly wanted this acknowledgement.

Though no general cartel was reached, Howe had learned that his request to resign his command had been approved, and remained interested in exchanging as many of his men as possible. Thus some hundreds of prisoners were exchanged in May and June 1778, before the British evacuated Philadelphia on June 18.

By this time Boudinot was anxious to leave the position and take his seat in Congress. Though he recommended one of his deputies, William Atlee of Lancaster, to succeed him, Congress ignored this recommendation. The position was offered to someone else, without consulting the prospective office holder, who refused it. Boudinot was eventually succeeded in office by Major John Beatty of New Jersey who served until 1780. The Commissary of Prisoners operation remained largely as Boudinot, the first office holder, had established it until 1780 when Congress implemented major reforms.

Joseph Lee Boyle   Birdsboro, Pennsylvania

EDITORIAL PROCEDURE

The letterbook is in Boudinot's hand which is often very small and cramped. The spelling and grammar are much rougher than in his surviving signed letters. This publication presents a literal transcription with spelling, punctuation and grammar remaining as they are found in the original. The writer's abbreviations and contractions are also preserved as they are found in the manuscript.

Capital letters follow the text of the originals, although it is sometimes a guess whether a letter is a capital or not. Brackets indicate questionable or illegible letters and words. *Sic* is used very sparingly as it would quickly detract from the text, given the numerous variants of spelling and oddities of expression.

Letters are introduced by the names of the addressee. The dateline falls just below the heading, though the original document may have it at the bottom. The complimentary close is brought up flush with the last paragraph. A descriptive note at the foot of each entry identifies the recipient the first time each individual appears.

All names are spelled as found in the manuscript, though corrected where known, in the index. In some cases similar names, such as Captains Keeting and Keating, are probably the same individual, though this is not completely certain from the text. Other names are similar in spelling but are definitely two individuals, such as Major William Edmestone of the 48th Regiment of Foot and Major Charles Edmonstone of the 18th Regiment of Foot.

While most of the letters appear chronologically in the letterbook, some were out of place. In this publication they are arranged in chronological order. Crossed out material is shown in italics. Margin notes are shown as postscripts, except where obviously keyed to the body of the document.

The index includes the names of all persons. However place names are selected, depending on relevance and frequency. Casual references to New York, for example, have been omitted.

To the Governors and Executive Bodies of the Thirteen States

May it please your Exc^y—   Morris Town [N. J.] 17 Ap^l. 1777
    Being honored with the appointment of Commissary General of Prisoners in the Army of the united States of America, it is absolutely necessary that I should be immediately provided with an Account of all the Expences and disbursements of the different States in favour of the several Prisoners taken from the King of Great Brittain, in order that the Accounts may be ready for Settlement with General Howe, whenever we should be called upon for that purpose—I am therefore instructed by his Exc^y Genl. Washington to beg the favour of your Exc^y. to order all Acc^{ts}. of Expences & disbursements (as well those that have already been paid, as those which are yet due) made by your State in favour of such Prisoners, to be immediately transmitted to me at Head Quarters, with the several proper authenticated Vouchers for the same—I must also beg a return of such Prisoners as are at present in your State, with the particular Places where confined, their Ranks &c
    I have the honor to be &c
The above sent to all the Gov^{rs}. & Executive Bodies of the 13 united States, mutatis mentendo with Titles &c

To the Secretary of the Board of War

Sir,   Morris Town [N.J.] Aprill 17 1777
    Having the Honor of the Appointment of Commissary Genl. of Prisoners in the Army of the united States of america, I am instructed by his Exc^y. Genl. Washington to desire the favour of your Board; directing such Extracts from the resolutions of Congress, as relate to this department if any, to be made out & transmitted to me at Head Quarters for my Government there [under]—His Exc^y. has directed me to appoint Deputies in the different States [unless appointments] for this Matter has been otherwise directed by Congress—
    I am &—

At this time Richard Peters was Secretary of the Board of War.

To Joshua Loring

Sir   Morris Town [N.J.] Aprill 30th. 1777

Being honored with the Appointment of Commissary General of Prisoners in the Army of the united States of America, I am instructed to acknowledge the receipt of your Letters of the 24 March & 8th. Aprill to his Exc^y. General Washington, enclosing the returns of Prisoners exchanged, and of those Officers who had deserted from their Paroles—I have express directions to assure you that it is with the most particular dissatisfaction, that his Exc^y the Commander in Chief hears that any Officer under his Command, should be so lost to every Sentiment of Virtue, as to violate their Faith & Honor, by deserting their Paroles, and had it [earlier] come to his Knowledge, or was it now in his Power, they would all attend this Flag on their return; but as their Time in the Service of the united States of America has been long expired, they have avoided Head Quarters, and we so suppose are dispersed to the different Places of their abode; but I am authorized to give you the strongest Assurances, that his Exc^y will take the most effectual Means to collect them together and if in his Power to accomplish it, will return them without any delay, but what will necessarily arise from their scattered Situation—The only Person in his Power, Ensign Hander of the Connecticut forces, returns with the present Flag, and the General would fair hope that this will be the last Instance in which you will have reason to complain of a Conduct so injurious to the Honor of the american Service.—At the same time give me leave Sir, to hint to you, that while his Exc^y the Commander in Chief, is thus endeavouring to enforce & inculcate the strictest attention & regard to the dictates of Honor & good Faith in the Officers under his Command, by obliging them to return to their several Paroles, he hopes they will not in the present Instance meet with any unnecessary Severity, as they have in a great Measure been encouraged by some of the British Officers, that have Dishonored themselves in the same unjustifiable manner, with regard to their Paroles, and who have not been treated with any undue rigor or Severity, and I cannot but here particularly take Notice of a Capt. M^c[Cay], who it is reported is again received into your Service, and Coll L[aree] of the new Levies, who I must also expect, will in like manner be returned to us—

I duly observe what you say relative to the Subsistence of our Officers with you, and shall endeavour for the future to supply them with every necessary, so as to prevent any such allowance—

In Answer to your request relating to Lt Coll. Greene, I am sorry to inform you of the difficulty attending the Matter, arising from the Circumstances of the Exchange—The French Gentlemen were sent in, last December when their particular Ranks were fixed & allowed, this was confirmed so long after as by the Exchange in March last, on the receipt whereof his Exc.^{y} did not hesitate to discharge Coll. Greene from his Parole—this was done previous to the receipt of yours of the 8th. Aprill—The General thinks the Mistake of a very extraordinary nature, after so long a Time had for Consideration and is extremely sorry that any difficulty should arise on this Occasion, but conceives you must be sensible, that is has not arose from any default of his—

I have the Honor to be &

P.S.

Since writing the above we are informed that the Hon^{le}. John Fell Esqr. of Bergen County is a Prisoner with you, it would be exceedingly agreeable to me Sir, if the Exchange of M^{r}. Fell could be had for any of the Gentlemen now on their Parole in New York, as M^{ssr} Wallace, Philips, or Jauncey—If this should be acceptable to you, I will immediately either of those Gentlemen's Parole to be ready for this Purpose—

Loring was Commissary General of Prisoners with the British forces. He was then located in New York City.

To Joshua Loring

Sir,   Morris Town [N.J.] May 8 1777

The enclosed Letter I sent you last Week via Staten Island, attended by Ensign Hander in Consequence of your Letter of the 8 ulitmo, but to my great surprize the Flag was returned by the officer there without assigning any reason that I have heard of—I am at a Loss to know whether it was occasioned by Place sent to, being disagreeable to the Gent^{n} commanding there—the

The rest of this letter and the first part of the next, are missing from the letterbook.

To Lewis Pintard

who have come out, complain that they have great injustice done them with regard to their Board, by reason that the Inhabitants are not paid the two Dollars p^r week allowance—This is not the Case here, as I have p^d large Sums for different British Officers, who have been suffered to return on being exchanged & out of Cash without any reimbursements—There is a John Gibbons, a Private who was take at Borden Town and Joel Westcott 1st. Lieu^t. in Capt. Wests Company of Coll L. Cadwalladers reg^t whose familiars are very anxious to hear from them—If you could let me know how they are, it would be very agreeable to their Friends—

I enclose you a number of Letters for different Prisoners and the following Sums of money—£22:7 in Jersey Bills for Thos. Lambert Byles—a Capt at Long Island—two half Jos & two Silver Dollars for Lieu^t. Andrew Boyd—two half Jos & three Silver Dollars & one English Shilling for David Brooks—five half Jos. for Lieu^t. Henry Shoemaker Lieu^t. John Kelly 6 Guineas—John Stockton 3 half Johs.—all which I must beg your particular Care to deliver to them—

I forgot to mention to you, that the several Officers who are returned with this Flag, have also rec^d sufficient Cloathing here for the Present—
Am &c
P.S. All the Keys in my House were taken away, as they could not be of any Advantage to any Person, I rather think S. Francis has them, I wish you would enquire & let me know—The Deeds for the House you bought of M^r. Tennent are found, so that matter is safe—

Lewis Pintard had been appointed as an agent of the Continental Congress to care for American prisoners in the New York City area. "Jos" or "Johs" were an abbreviation for the Johannes, a Portugese coin then in common use.

To Joshua Loring

Sir   Morris Town [N.J.] May 22^d 1777
I wrote you on the 5th. Instant which I hope you have rec^d. altho' not favoured with an Answer—This is attended by Lieu^t. M^{ac}Clure, Lieu^t. Henry Shoemaker Lieu^t. Jacob Mummey, Ensign W^m. Lowther Charles Willson—who are returned by order of his Exc^y. Genl. Washington having deserted from their Paroles—They assure me that they were induced to

this dishonorable piece of Conduct by being unjustly suspected of intending to come off and threatened with Confinement in Consequence— I am sorry the distresses of our Prisoners whould tempt them to this unjustifiable measure, but hope the Gen[ls] fixed Determination of returning every Man who comes away without being regularly exchanged, will put a stop to it, without obliging you to any rigor or Severity—
Am &c

To Joshua Loring

Sir,   Morris Town [N.J.] May 26 1777
By a Letter just rec[d]. from M[r]. Lewis Pintard (forwarded by you)— returning the appointment of deputy Commissary of Prisoners I had sent him, am informed "that he cannot hold that appointment and believes that no Person bearing the like Commission would be permitted to remain in New York, but that he would be permitted to receive Provisions and any other necessaries for our Prisoners and distribute the same—That he was also desired to inform me, that it will now be expected that full Supplies be sent in, for all the Prisoners now with you, and for all such as may hereafter be taken"—As it is not to be doubted bur that M[r]. Pintard was properly authorized to make this Representation, I am instructed to desire of you, a full & clear Explanation of General Howe's Expectations & resolutions with regard to the future Subsistance of our Prisoners—It is a Matter of the greatest Consequence that this important Article should be well understood on each side of the Question, that unnecessary Trouble to ourselves as well as distress to those, whom the fortune of war may render Prisoners, may be timely prevented—When M[r]. Pintard was sent to New York, it was on purpose to know, if he might be permitted to remain there as our Commissary of Prisoners taken by the British Army, in a manner similar to that which M[r]. Franks was allowed to execute among us, in favour of the Prisoners taken by the American Army—By your Answer of the 8th. Ultmo, Gen[l]. Washington was informed that "there were no Objections to the employing of M[r]. Pintard or any other Person in furnishing the Prisoners with Provisions, or any other necessary Articles we might be desirous of sending in to them"—After this Acquiescence it was not doubted, but that the request was granted and that M[r]. Pintard would have the same Priveledge of supplying our Prisoners with Prisoners with Provisions, as M[r]. Franks enjoyed with us, and also of distributing

whatever might be sent into them—Hereupon I immediately forwarded M^r. Pintards appointment with Bills of Exchange to the amount of £600 Sterl. towards an immediate supply, not supposing that it could have been expected, we should employ a Person in so important a Trust without a formal Appointment—His Excellency Genl. Washington, as well as every impartial man, must think it very extraordinary that while your Officers (Prisoners with us) are at Liberty to demand an Allowance of two Dollars p^r Week from us, and your Soldiers with their Wives & Children receive the most ample Supply of Provision of the same Quality with that rec^d. by our own Troops—That when an Agent of the Contractors for Victualling the british Troops is allowed to negotiate Bills of Exchange at an [advanc]ed Pr[emium] and thence to supply both Officers and Soldiers with Provisions & other necessaries at his Pleasure purchased here; and in many Instances your Officers when out of Cash, suffered to return to you on being exchanged without any reimbursement of the Subsistence rec^d. by them, and even monies advanced for the Transportation of themselves, their Wives, Children, Servants & Baggage and that notwithstanding all this, there should now arise any [obstruc]tion to the admitting, or objection to the appointment of a proper Person to superintend & supply our Prisoners in the same manner, as we permit M^r. Franks to supply yours—If the Person appointed by us is not allowed to purchase any necessaries among your Inhabitants for the Prisoners it must be in vain to forward Supplies of Cash to them, as the same Objections must lay ag^t. their purchasing for themselves as ag^t. another's purchasing for them—M^r. Pintard refers me to a Letter he expected you would write me, by the same Conveyance you forwarded his—had you wrote, perhaps these difficulties might have been so explained as to have prevented the necessity of any farther Application, as well as informed us of your Intentions with regard to the Exchange of M^r. Fell mentioned in my last to you, which is yet without an Answer—I doubt not but that you will see the necessity, as well as the propriety of having this Interesting Point with regard to the Subsistence of Prisoners [work]ed to some certain and comprehensive Rules, as the same Line of Conduct towards your Prisoners with us, will for the future be strictly & resolutely pursued—If you should think proper still to persist in the Article of a full supply being sent in from us to our Prisoners; you will be so kind as to fix the day from which so extraordinary a Circumstance is to take Place on our part, as it will from that Time be expected, that the same Measure will be pursued by you, with regard to the Prisoners with us—

I am under a necessity of mentioning that a number of Officers of your Army have been sent in, under their Paroles, to exchange our Officers of equal rank, otherwise to return & surrender themselves to Genl. Washington, and altho' they have been a long Time with you, neither Alternative has been as yet complied with—Some of those Gent^n. are, if my memory serves me, Capt. Gamble, Ensign A. Campbell, Commissary M^{ac}Cullough & Commissary M^{ac}Intosh, with several others whose Names I will transmit in my next—These two last Gent^n have been taken Prisoners & sent in twice—There are also several Surgeons who are with you on Parole, any one of which I should be glad to exchange for D^r. M^{ac}Henry, who is at Philadelphia on his Parole from you—

I am &c

To Lewis Pintard

Dr Sir   Morris Town [N.J.] May 26 1777
Your favour of the 19th. Inst^t. returning your Appointm^t as Commissary of Prisoners, came safe to hand. I should have glad you had stated the objections that were made to your holding that appointment, after Genl. Howe's acquaintance therein, and for which Purpose your Application was expressly made—I could wish this matter was put on a proper footing, or at least that the objections to it, may be satisfactory, as your remaining with your family may depend upon it—It would have been more agreeable had I rec^d. an Answer from Mr Loring as you expected, which might have removed several difficulties that at present appear to be raised without much foundation; but he has not thought proper to give any Answer as yet, even to my request ab^t. M^r. Fell—I should be glad you would acquaint me of his Health &c for the sake of his Family—I wrote you a few days before the rec^t. of your last, in which I considered you as acting under the Appointment and transmitted the 2^d. Bill of Exchange and now enclose the third—I also send in some hard money for several Prisoners, all under cover to M^r. Loring, in which way I allways send your Letters—

I had no Idea that the monies sent in to the Prisoners was to go towards payment of their Board (I mean the allowance of 2 Dollars p^r week) as no such deduction, as far as has come within my Knowledge, is made with us, untill an Exchange takes Place; and often then it is dispensed with—As to sending in Provisions for the support of our

Prisoners, I imagine the same line of Conduct will be pursued, as is used towards the british Prisoners with us, but the sending a Surplus for the Purchase of other necessaries, I can hardly think will be admitted as the transmitting Cash will be attended with so much less trouble; and if there are any substantial Objections ag^t purchasing with hard Money, they must lay in equal force ag^t. purchasing at any rate whatever—However I will take the advice of Congress on the Subject & proceed accordingly—I am curious to know what Quantity of Cloaths are wanted and to what Places it will be most proper to forward them, which I expected to have response from M^r. Loring before this—I have wrote him fully on this Subject of the future Subsistence of Prisoners—I am really sorry that the difficulties attending the unhappy dispute should be unnecessarily increased—we are well &c

Am &c

To Richard Peters

Sir   June 16 1777 Middle brook [N.J.]

In the hurry of a general movement, I can only say that I am obliged to forward Seven Prisoners of War as p^r return enclosed, to the Care of the Board of War, to be sent to Lancaster—

By my Commission from Genl. Washington, I am authorized to appoint as many Deputies, as I think the Service requires; in Consequence whereof I should have appointed one in Philadelphia, had not the Board of War hinted, that two were sufficient, one at Lancaster & the other at Massachusetts Bay—Since this I am convinced that the Service must suffer unless more are appointed, especially one at Philadelphia and one with each grand division of the Army to the Eastward & Northward—No one who has not made the Experiment can easily conceive the amazing Expence attending Prisoners of War being sent on to different Places or the difficulty in keeping clear Accounts & vouchers of their Expences, without proper Persons to attend to them in the different Places where it is necessary they should be sent—I have lately rec^d from the Clerk of the Congress, Copies of the Resolutions made since the Commencement of the War relating to my department, among wch. is one requesting each State to appoint a Commissary of Prisoners of War—This resolution militates directly ag^t. my Appointment, as there is an absolute Necessity while we are obliged to keep our Acc^{ts}. & Vouchers, so as to settle with

the Enemy, that the Office should finally center in one Man—
Am &

To The President of the Convention of New York

Sir   June 19 Middlebrook [N.J.]
By order of his Exc^y. Genl. Washington I lately made Application to the Commissary of Prisoners in the british Army for an Exchange of the Honble. John Fell Esqr. one of the Counsellors of this State, for Messrs. Wallace, Philips or Ja[nne]ly sent in to the Enemy on their Parole by Govr. Trumbull—I rec^d for Answer that Genl. Howe would not admit of the Exchange—In Consequence of this Answer, by the advice of the Board of War of the order of Genl. Washington, I have wrote this Day to Govr. Trumbull to order a return of all those Persons belonging to your State who were sent in on their Paroles by his Honor, and that your State would be ready to receive, secure & provide for them in a proper Manner—
You will therefore be pleased to take proper Measures for this Purpose on their arrival in Connecticut, lest they may consider themselves as discharged from their Paroles & affect an Escape—This Application to you is in Consequence of Copies of Letters lately transmitted to me by the Board of War, that passed between your Convention & Govr Trumbull on the subject of these Prisoners whereby in appears they are properly Prisoners of your State—
Am &

To Jonathan Trumbull

Sir   Middle Brook [N.J.] June 19 1777
By order of his Exc^y the Commander in Chief, I lately made Application to the Commissary of Prisoners of the british Army for the Exchange of the hon^ble John Fell Esqr a Counsellor of this State (lately made a Prisoners by the Tories from the County of Bergen) for Mr Wallace or any of their other Counsellors lately sent in to the Enemy on their Paroles by your Honor from your State—I have rec^d. for Answer that Genl. Howe did not admit of the Exchange—In Consequence whereof, I am desired by his Exc^y to request that you will be pleased to order all those Persons, belonging to the State of New York who are on

Parole to your Honor, immediately to return, where that State will take care that they are properly secured and provided for according to their different Ranks—I should be much obliged by having the Acc^ts of Expences incurred by your State on acc^t. of Prisoners of War as also a return of such as are yet with you, agreeable to my former Letter to your Honor—Should be glad of an Acc^t of the officers who have broke their Paroles with you—their ranks, Corps & whether retaken or not, since the Commencement of the War, as the Enemy deny the Fact.

Am &

Trumbull was Governor of Connecticut.

To The President of The Council of Massachusetts Bay

Sir   Middlebrook [N.J.] June 19 1777
Being lately informed by Congress of their resolve for building Barracks in your State for keeping Prisoners of War, I must beg the favour of you to let me know as speedily as possible in what forwardness they are in, where building, and when you think it is likely they will be fit to receive the Prisoners, as the Congress are very anxious to have them formed into proper Arrangements—I wrote you some time ago for an Account of the Expences your State have been at, on Acc^t. of Prisoners of War, and also a return of those in your State, both which, I should be glad of being favoured with as soon as can be with any Conveniency—

Am &

To David Franks

Sir,   Camp at Middlebrook [N.J.] June 28 1777
Enclosed I send you a Letter to Sergeant George M^acKay of the 42^d. Regim^t. at Lancaster, and by this Conveyance, also a Bag of necessaries sealed with a Seal containing the Impression of a Cupid & two Hearts— this Bag was sent to me from Coll Sterling and a Handkerchief of Cloaths for Serg Stone from the Adjutant of Queens Regim^t. of light Dragoons— You have all herewith a Hogshead containing as I am informed, the Cloaths & other necessaries mentioned in Sergeant M^acKay's Letter for the use of the British Prisoners in Lancaster—I have also rec^d Thirty one Guineas for british Prisoners which I shall forward you, as soon as I can

get an Opportunity I can trust—You will be pleased to acknowledge the receipt of the Hogshead & Bag &c

Am Sir &c

P.S. I have also 28 Guineas left, belonging to the 16 Reg^t. of light Dragoons. I have already paid those who are at Lancaster, but cannot tell where the others are quartered—If you know pray acquaint me with it—I would be obliged to you for a return of all the Prisoners you supply.

Franks, an American at Philadelphia, had been appointed an agent to care for British and Hessian prisoners. After the British Army occupied Philadelphia in September 1777, he remained in the city and provided assistance to the American prisoners held there.

To Richard Peters

Sir   Camp M. Brook [Middlebrook, N.J.] June 30 1777

By order of his Excellency the Commander in Chief, I enclose a Copy of a Letter, rec^d this Morning by him, from Coll Magaw, in order that the Board of War may be possessed of every Information relative to our unhappy Prisoners in Possession of the Enemy—Their Distress is almost intolerable, and seems to be greatly heightened by the apparent neglect with which they have been treated—The Enemy seem to be doing every Thing in their Power to prevent their relief. We were first assured that Bills of Exchange would answer as well as Cash; now they cannot be negotiated—From M^r. Pintard's Silence on this Subject, I rather think that he is prevented from writing his Sentiments especially as on rec^t. of the Bill, he had no doubt of disposing of it at 82 ½ p^r C^t—I could most heartily wish the Specie, I had reason to expect from the secret Committee long ago, could have been forwarded: It has been said here, that there is a large Sum in Specie, left from the northern Expedition; if so, it could not be laid out better, than to save a parcell of the bravest of Men from Destruction—

From what the General has informed me, I expected Instructions from the Board of War, relative to a Contract to be made with M^r. Loring in favor of the Prisoners on both Sides—However as I knew great delay would inevitably happen, and the resolutions of Congress being on a broad Bottom, I have ventured to break the matter to M^r. Loring, that I may have some Answer, by the Time I receive the Instructions—Part of the Cloaths ordered for the Prisoners last Aprill, has just come to hand from the Clothier General, the remainder I am soliciting from Morris Town—If any Thing more can be done for our suffering Bretheren, I must earnestly beg your utmost exertions in their Behalf, that no unnecessary Delay may increase their misfortunes.

Am &c

To David Franks

Sir,   Camp M. Brook [Middlebrook, N.J.] June 30th 1777
    By the Bearer Coll. Biddle, I send you 31 Guineas, 29 of which are for the Privates &c of the 42[d]. Regim[t]. of british Troops now at Lancaster, as p[r] list enclosed to you last week in a Letter to Sergeant M[ac]Kay—The remaining two are for Sergeant Stone of the light Dragoons in your City, a Letter to whom from the Cornet of his Company, I also enclose you, with the Cloaths & necessaries for the same Corps, sent you via Trenton—Be so kind as to acknowledge the receipt of the whole, and when you pay the Men, they must mention in their rec[ts]. of their having rec[d] it in Specie—

    I am &c

To Robert Richards

Sir,   Camp M. B. [Middlebrook, N.J.] June 30th 1777
    I have authority from Congress to appoint a Deputy Com. Gen[l] of Prisoners in the Army of the United States of America, to be resident in the City of Philadelphia—His Business will be to receive such Prisoners of War as are or shall be sent to that City from whatever Quarter, take a particular Acc[t]. of their Names, Corps, when & where taken, and forward them on as he shall be directed by me or any superior Officer: Also to make such Purchases of Provision & other necessaries as may be wanted for the Supply of Prisoners of War that may be under my Care—The Trouble will be trifling, as the Commanding Officer of the City must provide their proper Guards & the Barrack Master their proper Quarters—The Pay & Rations are that of a Major which is 50 Dollars p[r] Month & 4 Rations p[r] Day—Thus I have given a concise Sketch of the duty required; and now permit me (as it may be an Amusement to you) to ask if you or M[r] Searle will accept of it—your immediate answer will be very agreeable. Am &c

Richards must not have been interested in the job as there is no additional correspondence to him.

To James Mease

Sir,   Camp M. B. [Middlebrook, N.J.] June 30 1777
    I am to acknowledge the rec^t. of your favour of the 18th. Inst^t. attended with the Cloathing for the use our Prisoners in New York—I have wrote to M^r. Young for the Shirts, but can get no Answer from him—I expect to go to Morris Town to morrow on purpose, as the necessity is very great—
    Am &c

Mease, then located in Philadelphia, was Clothier General for the Continental Army.

To Lewis Pintard

D^r. Sir,   Camp MB. [Middlebrook, N.J.] July 1st 1777
    It is long since I have had a line for you, and am anxious to hear how you & the family are—I enclose you to the Care of M^r. Loring, 14 half Johannes and three Guineas for Lieu^t. Coll Thomas Bull on Long Island—and one half Joh. one Guinea & five Dollars for Capt W^m. Scott which I beg you will deliver as speedily as possible as they are in great want of it—we are all well as when I wrote last—you will soon hear from me again as the Prisoners Cloaths are on the road—
    Am &c

To Robert Magaw

D^r. Sir,   Camp M Brook [Middlebrook, N.J.] July 1st. 1777
    At the request of the Board of War,* I must beg the favour of you to send out to me, the best return of your Regim^t. at the Time it was taken, that is in your Power, particularizing, the Dead, those taken Prisoner and such who escaped by Absence or otherwise—The Distresses of our Prisoners give the greatest uneasiness to all your Friends here, and you may depend upon it, that every possible measure is taking for your speedy

relief and you will hereafter, I hope find, that you have not been forgotten
Am &c
[Boudinot Notes] *This ought to have been, the Treasury Board—

Magaw was Colonel of the Fifth Pennsylvania Regiment. He had been taken prisoner at
Fort Washington in November 1776, and was being held on Long Island, New York.

To Robert Lettis Hooper

Sir   Morris Town [N.J.] July 5 1777
As there are Prisoners of War frequently forw^d. on to Lancaster by
way of Easton, and it is not worth while, going to the Expence of a Stated
Commissary for the purpose of providing them with Provisions there, I
must beg the favour of you to take the Trouble of overseeing & supplying
such Prisoners of War, as may be sent to your Care from time to time, and
I will not only account with you for the Expence but also reward you for
the Trouble you may be put to on this occasion—You will be pleased to
forw^d. on such Prisoners of War as are now at Easton to Lancaster,
without distinction of Corps &c
Am &c

Hooper, at Easton, Pennsylvania, was serving as a Deputy Quarter Master General, and
also served as Deputy Commissary General of Prisoners.

To James Wilson and Christian Forster

Gent^n.   Camp at Morris Town [N.J.] July 5 1777
As humanity to Prisoners of War has ever been the peculiar
Characteristic of the american Army, notwithstanding the many improper
returns we have received from the Subjects of it, the Genl. exceedingly
regrets the necessity he is sometimes reduced to, of exerting himself to
prevent the abuse of that Liberty, with which the Prisoners have been
indulged—When you parted with his Exc^y he reminded you of the
necessity of a prudent Behaviour under your present Circumstances, and is
now very sorry that it had not such an Effect, as to prevent the many
Complaints from the Neighbourhood of your Quarters, which he has rec^d.
of your imprudent Conduct, in some Instances in violation of your
Paroles—

It is hoped that by this you will be reminded to keep a stricter Guard on your own Conduct, as you will never be indulged with another hint of this kind in future—The Bearer Lieu^t. Minnis will wait on you to Philadelphia on your Way to Lancaster County, to such Place there as the Board of War will direct you, whether it is his Exc^y. Pleasure that you repair & abide—As the Paroles you signed to Genl. Sullivan, are not agreeable to the prescribed form, I have sent them by the Bearer to be returned when you sign those he will produce to you of the same Tenor—
Am &

Wilson and Forster, then prisoners of war, were Lieutenants in the British Fifty-Fifth Regiment of Foot.

To William Gordon

Rev^d. & Dr Sir   Camp at Morris Town [N.J.] July 9th. 1777
     Being lately appointed Commissary General of Prisoners in the Army of the united States of America, there has been added to the office by his Excellency the General, the duty of Collecting Intelligence for the use & Information of the Commander in Chief—Shall I my D^r. Sir presume upon the short acquaintance I have been honored with by you, to ask the favour of your Correspondence for this purpose—I know of no Person who can be of more essential Service on this occasion, than yourself, The Bearer Joshua Mesereaw Esqr. my Deputy Commissary of Prisoners for the State of Massachusets Bay, will deliver this—He is a man of probity & Character and can give you as good an account of all our late movements as any man in the Army
     It is generally expected here that our course will be Eastward, perhaps towards Provedence, but all these matters are yet secrets,—

Gordon was a clergyman in Massachusetts.

To The President of the State of Massachusets Bay

Sir   Camp Morris Town [N.J.] July 9th 1777
     The Bearer Joshua Messereau Esqr. deputy Commissary of Prisoners, will wait on you with this,—I must in behalf of the Service beg your assistance for him, in obtaining an exact State of the Prisoners of War with

you, He has also Instructions for enquring into the State of the Barracks lately ordered to be built under your derections for the reception of Prisoners of War—If they are not finished and he can be of any assistance in pushing them forward he will do it with pleasure—He is a man of understanding in this way, and of great Probity—As we are not without hopes of an Exchange of Prisoners yet taking place, Suffer me Sir to hint the necessity of our being furnished with Proper Acco^{ts} of Expences & disbursements of your State in behalf of Prisoners of War

To Jonathan Trumbull

Sir   Camp Morris Town [N.J.] July 9th. 1777
    The Bearer Joshua Messereau Esqr. deputy Commissary of Prisoners, will wait on your Excellency with this—
    I shall take it as a particular favour, if your would afford him the necessary Assistance in obtaining proper Accounts of the Prisoners of War, in your State—
    As we are not yet without hopes that some kind of an Exchange will take Place, I must urge to your Excellency the necessity of expediting of the Expenditure of your State in Behalf of Prisoners

To John Adam

    By Virtue of the Powers & Authority to me given by the Congress of the United Stated of America, for the purpose—I do hereby nominate, constitute and appoint, you the said John Adam, deputy Commissary General of Prisoners in the Army of the United States of America—And you are hereby required to do and perform all and every Service Matter & Thing relating to and concerning the said Office of Deputy Commissary General in the said Army Accordingly, and that for and during my Pleasure, as witness my hand and seal this Eighth Day of July Anno Domini 1777

Adam served as Deputy Commissary General of Prisoners at Fishkill, New York.

Instructions for John Adam Esq[r]. deputy
Commissary of Prisoners in the Army of The
United States of America—July 9 1777

1st. You are to repair to the Eastern Division of the Army of the united States of America, now under the Command of Major General Putnam, and there wait on the Gen[l]. and acquaint him with your appointment—The Quarter Master General will give you proper Quarters

2[d]. You are to apply to the General, to get proper Orders issued for Obliging Returns to be made you of all Prisoners of War either taken from or by our Army under his Command particularizing their Names, Corps, Time when & place where taken—as soon as such return is made (of those taken by us) you are to take Charge of such Prisoners, and see that they are committed immediately to the Provost Guard, and Supplyed with Provision from the Issuing Commissary, till they are sent of to their proper destination

3[d] Whenever you send off any Number of Prisoners, they are to go under a proper Guard, to be provided by the Adjutant Gen[l]. and you are to make out proper returns, Containing the several particulars as above together with the place where sent to, one of which you are to send with the Prisoners and the other keep yourself, or rather have it in a Book and once every month transmit me a general return of the whole

4. You are to keep very exact Accounts of all Expences & Disbursements relating to your department, with proper vouchers for every Charge a state of which is also to be transmitted to me once a month

5th. Whenever a Commissioned Officer is taken you are to take his Parole in the Form prescribed (Unless otherwise ordered by the Commanding Officer of the Army) and forward him on under the Care of an Officer of equal Rank—If a Number are together, then of the Rank of the highest Officer who is prisoner—

6. Untill Barracks are ready to Receive Prisoners of War (which I hope will soon be) you are to send them to such Places as shall be directed by the General or other Command[g]. Officer of the Division

7. You are not to suffer any Person to be Exchanged, but for a Prisoner of ours of equal rank and that has been longest in Captivity, unless you are expressly ordered to the Contrary

8th. You are to keep a Constant Eye to gaining Intelligence from every Quarter, for which no expence is to be spared; and you are not to loose an oppertunity of keeping me will informed of every Circumstance that passes and of every piece of Intelligence that can be gained, at the same time attending particularly to the authenticity of it, so that I may not be misled

9th. Whenever you want Money for Immediate Service you are to call on the General who will give you a Warrant for the Necessary Sum on Acco^t. of the Paymaster; an Acco^t. of which you are to transmit to me as before

10 No Officer who is Prisoner with us, is to be exchanged untill he Clears off all his Debts & Expences for Board &c

11th I am to be advised of all Exchanges, with their particular Circumstances

To Joshua Mersereau

Instructions for Joshua Mesereau Esqr. deputy Commissary Genl. of Prisoners for the State of Massachusets Bay, he having rec^d a Commission therefore of the same Tenor with the one preceding to John Adam Esqr.—July 9th. 1777

1st. You are without Delay to proceed to the State of Connecticut and there call on Govr. Trumbull, and endeavour to obtain some State of the Prisoners of War in Connecticut—particularizing their Names, Corps Times when & Places where taken and where they now reside—You are also to send me an Acc^t. how they are now provided for, by whom and at what rate—Your will also represent to his Exc^y. the Govr. the necessity of my having the Acc^{ts}. of all Expences on behalf of Prisoners of War, without delay—

2^d. From thence you are to the nearest Place you can obtain proper Intelligence relating to the Barracks that are building by order of Congress for the reception of Prisoners of War, in the State of Massachusets Bay— You are to consult with the Government there, and do all in your Power to hurry on the finishing of that Building, and if required by the President of the State, do you undertake the overseeing of the same—Endeavour to get the like State of the Prisoners of War in that State, as in Connecticut and also urge the forwarding the State of the Acc^{ts}. &c—

3^d. Enquire of the President of the Massachusets Bay, what Guards, or if any, will be appropriated for the use of the Barracks when finished and what N^o of Prisoners they will contain—also consult with him or the Councill where it will be best to sent the Officers, on their Parole, so as to separate them from the Privates—

4. As you go thro' the Eastern States, you are to endeavour to secure

some few Stores of Rum, Sugar, Tea, Coffee &c and also some dry Goods if to be had at a reasonable rate, in order to be ready to supply the Prisoners of War, as I am about contracting for the mutual supply of Prisoners—whatever monies you may want, draw on me for at 20 Days sight or sooner if you find it necessary, and the Bills shall be duly paid—
5. If you find the Barracks ready to receive the Prisoners, advise me of it without delay and wait my Answer before you return—
6 At all times you are to lay yourself out as far as possible to gain the best Intelligence in your Power, keeping me well & speedily advised by every Opportunity, as well by Post as otherwise—
7th. If you go to Boston, call on the Rev^d. M^r. Gordon near Boston with the Letters herewith, and endeavour to establish a Correspondence with him & myself, as also with every Person on you Way, who may appear to you, to be calculated for the Purpose of gaining Intelligence—
8 Endeavour to make Acquaintance by the way if possible, with proper Persons who may in Case the Army should move Eastward, answer for the purpose of sending out to gain Intelligence—
9th If you go to Boston you are to wait on the Commander of the Continental Army and acquaint him with your Appointment & take his Commands
10th. Enquire in the State of Connecticut for the Prisoners of the 16 Reg^t of light Dragoons—let them know that I have 36 Guineas for them to be distributed as p^r list sent herewith—If they will let me know to whom I shall forward there, I will send them without delay—if they will take Currency for them & will desire it as a favour you may pay them at 100 p^r C^t—

Mersereau served as Deputy Commissary General of Prisoners in Massachusetts.

To Lewis Pintard

D^r. Sir   Pumpton [Pompton, N.J.] July 10th. 1777
By this Conveyance I forward on to you 100 Suits of Cloaths for our Prisoners with you, as Pr Invoice enclosed, which I must beg you will distribute in the best manner you can to the most necessitous, and acquaint me with the number that will yet be wanted, distinguishing between Officers & Soldiers—I also send the following sums money—For Jaques Voorhise a lame Man carried off from Somerset Ten half Joh^s. for Phil. Folkerson from same place, two half Johs.—For Jos. King one half Joh. &

Six Dollars—For Capt; Schott of Coll. Armand's Legion Six Guineas & two for the Soldiers taken with him—for Chas. Willson & W^m. Lowther two Dollars. Besides the above I also send a Portmanteau &c for Capt. John Lowrie—a parcell of Cloaths for Jaques Voorhise—The same for Phil: Folkerson and a Bundle for Jos: King—I would be much obliged by being informed of the Health of one Jona^n. Hager a Soldier or whether he is dead or alive—you have a Letter enclosed for him—

 Am &

On July 11 the Continental Army moved to Pompton Plains, New Jersey, eighteen miles northeast of Morristown.

To Charles Gordon

Sir

 Yours of the 12th. Inst^t. to his Exc^y. Genl. Washington relative to your being permitted to go into New York has been referred by the Genl. to me as falling properly within my department—As his Exc^y has ever made it the invariable rule of his Conduct since he has had the Command of the American Army, to mitigate & soften the unavoidable distresses of war, whenever in his Power & consistant with his Duty to the Publick—I am instructed to signify his Pleasure that you be admitted on rec^t. hereof to proceed to the City of New York, first giving your Parole to the Councill of the State or the nearest Commanding Officer of the Continental Forces, in such Form as shall be prescribed by them, and that you will within two weeks after your arrival in New York, send out an Officer of equal Rank, who was captivated by the British Troops in Canada at the Three Rivers—or if none such are now in New York to be exchanged, then one, who has been longest in Captivity, and in Case of failure, that you return to the present State of your Confinement—It is expected that whatever allowance you have rec^d. or Debts you have Contracted since your Captivity will be previously discharged—It gives me Pleasure to be the means of gratifying you on this Occasion & hope you will return the favour by serving any of our Prisoners, when in your Power—

 Am &c

Gordon, a prisoners of war, was a Lieutenant in the British Seventy-First Regiment of Foot. He was then at Dunstable, Massachusetts.

To Richard Peters

Sir,   Pumpton [Pompton, N.J.] July 14 1777
    Agreeable to the resolve of Congress sent me in your last, I wrote to
M^r. Loring Com^y of Prisoners in the british Army, copy of which & his
Answer I enclose together with one rec^d. at some time from M^r. Pintard &
copies of mine to Loring previous to the above, which it seems has given
him offence—The reason for my troubling you with these Copies, is that
the Board of War may be possessed of every Thing that has passed
between us, by which they will see that the Enemy make use of every Shift
in their Power, to obstruct the intended relief for our unhappy Prisoners—
By M^r. Pintards Letter, you will observe the fate of the Bills of Exchange,
(which I also return) after a delay of upwards of 2 Months—I am
informed by the Bye, that these Bills would have been negotiated without
difficulty, could M^r. Loring have been prevailed upon, to have certifyed,
that they were for the use of the american Prisoners, but this he absolutely
refused, as is said—I refer it to the Board of War, if it would not be best
to return these Bills to the Drawer, & put a Stop to his drawing in future
for the Support of their Prisoners, but oblige them to send in Specie, as
they are now reducing us to the necessity of sending in Provision for the
support of ours—I shall as soon as we arrive at the North River send in
2000 Barrells of flour for their use (unless otherwise instructed by the
Board of War) tho' I must acknowledge it will be rather with reluctance,
as I know that the Enemy are in great want of that necessary Article—I
could wish to be informed whether money for the Prisoners had best be
sent me from your City, or whether it is expected that I shall draw it from
the Pay Master here—
    From a Conversation had between Coll Miles & his Exc^y. Genl.
Washington at which I was present, I understand that it is Genl. Howe's
wish to have an Exchange take Place, as to those who are now in
Captivity, without having any respect to the present dispute relative to
Genl. Lee and the Privates who died on the Road, before they reached the
Place of their destination—I am instructed by his Exc^y. to say that it is also
his wish that such an Exchange may take Place without any exception of
Coll Campbell or the Hessian field Officers, as he supposes that we shall
still have a sufficient Security in our Hands, from the surplus Privates that
will remain with us. As Coll. Miles is now in your City, he can fully explain
the whole matter—

I have at last given up any Expectation of obtaining Shirts for our unhappy Prisoners, and have therefore forwarded on the 100 Suits of Cloaths without Shirts, which I am afraid will greatly betray our Poverty—

You will observe by the number mentioned in M[r] Pintard's Last how inadequate this supply will be to their real wants; and I am sorry to say that Pumps being sent instead of Shoes, will lessen their usefullness—I must beg the favour of particular Instructions relating to the future Treatment of the british Prisoners with us, as I am clearly of opinion, that if we do not observe the same line of Conduct towards them as they have marked out relative to ours, they will be confirmed in their Opinion that we are afraid to act otherwise—You will undoubtedly observe that by M[r]. Franks being allowed to purchase Provision &c and draw Bills for Payment, at so enormous an Exchange, he supports the English Prisoners at a saving of at least 50 p[r] C[t]. while they are throwing every obstacle in the way to obstruct our supply and raise the Expence of it—

when I tell you that this Letter is wrote on a March with out scarcely a necessary for the purpose, and in the midst of a Crowd you will excuse every imperfection & make every candid allowance—

Am &c

P. S. On reflection, I do not know but the Bills of Exchange, ought to have been sent to the secret Committee, if so, must be the favour of you delivering them accordingly—I also enclose a curious Letter from a Coll. Barton of the new Levies to his wife, for publication—

To Henry Haller

Sir   Camp at the Clove [Smith's Clove, N.Y.] 22[d] July 1777

Being informed that by the dissolution of the Committee of your Committee of your County the Prisoners of War in the Town of Reading are left without any proper Person to take Charge of or oversee them, I am very desirous that proper Persons should be appointed to that necessary Business for the present, till matters relating to Prisoners of War in your State are put on a proper footing—As you have been recommended to me as fully qualified for this Purpose permit me to beg your undertaking the Office of deputy Commissary of Prisoners for your County for the Time being, lest an injury should arise to the publick Service by this accidental Circumstance of the Committee's dissolution—I enclose a short appointment to enable you to act in this Capacity and do engage to pay you such reasonable Compensation for your Trouble, as the Services you perform may be entitled to—

    I am &

By Virtue of the Powers & Authority to me committed for this Purpose I do hereby authorize, constitute and appoint Henry Haller Esqr. of the Town of Reading in the State of Pennsylvania, to act as deputy Commissary of Prisoners of War for the said Town [& area] to adjoined and as such to do & perform every act matter & thing appertaining to the duty of Commissaries of Prisoners of War untill farther Orders from me— As witness by Hand and Seal this 22^d July 1777

Henry Haller accepted the position of Deputy Commissary of Prisoners for Reading and the adjacent area. "The Clove" or "Smith's Clove," where the army had moved, was formed by the Ramapo River, which cut a broad, steep-sided valley through the southern flank of the rugged New York Highlands. Joseph Plumb Martin called it a "remarkable chasm in the mountains."

To Richard Peters

                    Camp at the Clove near New Windsor [Smith's Clove, N.Y.]
Dr Sir   July 22^d 1777
    Having been this moment informed by Letter from Reading in your State, that the Committee of that County is dissolved, and of Consequence the Prisoners of War there, are left without any Person to order or take Charge of them, I have thought it for the Service to authorize a Gent^n. there to act as Commissary of Prisoners pro tempore—This Gent^n. was recommended to me as the most proper Person for this Service, but as the Congress have limited the number of deputies, and I have promised this Gent^n. a reasonable recompence, I have enclosed my Letter to him that if the Board of War, think the measure unnecessary, they may stop it by destroying the Letter &c

    Am &

To Joseph Barton

Sir   Camp at the Clove [Smith's Clove, N.Y.] July 24 1777
By order of his Exc^y. the Commander in Chief, I am to acknowledge the receipt of your Letter directed to him relative to the Exchange of M^r. Pettit—I am instructed to inform you that his Exc^y cannot admit of any formal application of this kind, or enter into any Agreement for carrying your proposal into Execution but with an Officer having the Command of the district or Place from which he applies, and as you did not mention that you commanded on the Island, he waives an Answer untill the Application comes regularly from the Commanding Officer of Staten Island—

Barton, from Sussex County, New Jersey, was Lieutenant Colonel of a Loyalist regiment on Staten Island.

To David Franks

Letter of June 30 1777 recited
Sir   Camp at Clove [Smith's Clove, N.Y.] July 24 1777
The above is copy of what I wrote you of that Date, but the Gent^n. to whose Care I intrusted the Cash & Letter being prevented reaching your City, he would not trust it to any body else, and this afternoon returned them to me—I am sorry for the Delay, but hope it will not produce any bad Consequences—I have never recd any Thing whatever for Lieu^{ts}. Willson & Foster—
Am &

To William Livingston

Sir   Camp Peakskill [Peekskill, N.Y.] July 26 1777
I must beg the favour of you to get Permission of Genl. Putnam to go with a Flag to the Enemy's Lines, and make Application to the Commanding Officer of the British Troops for Passports for a Sloop load of flour going into New York to be delivered to Lewis Pintard Esqr. on Acc^t. of the american Prisoners there—She is under the Command of Jeremiah Wadsworth & two Men who will be under any Obligation that may be thought proper for their prudent Behaviour—I have already

permission from Genl Howe in a Letter from M^r. Loring, for the sending in Provisions by the way of Brunswick in the Jersey's, but the Situation of the Enemy being since altered & the Conveyance by the North River so much easier, it is necessary to made this Application—
    Am &

Livingston was Lieutenant Colonel of Webb's Additional Continental Regiment.

To Lewis Pintard

D^r. Sir   Camp Peakskill [Peekskill, N.Y.] July 27 1777
    I rec^d. your favour enclosing the Bills of Exchange & cannot but be surprized at the Treatment we receive on every Attempt to relieve our unhappy Prisoners—We are tolerably well informed of the means used to prevent this reasonable Proceeding in their Favour—That those Bills purchased of the british Agent, by which means he was furnished with Cash to answer his Purposes here with regard to the Enemies Troops with us, should be refused to be negotiated, is very extraordinary, especially as a Certificate from M^r. Loring of their being for the use of the american Prisoners would have obviated every Objection—However we must do, as we were done by—I send by the Sloop that takes this Letter 500 Barrells of Flour as p^r Invoice inclosed, which I must beg you will dispose of to the very best advantage & divide the neat Proceeds among our Prisoners—As soon as you possibly can, transmit me the Acc^t. Sales, that we may judge of the Propriety of forwarding a Quantity sufficient for the Purpose of [ful]ly supplying the demand of our Prisoners—I should be glad of your Opinion of the Quantity that will be requisite—The Person who has the Charge of this Sloop is Capt. Wadsworth who purchases the flour for me, and will take Care that it is good & delivered in proper Order.
    Be so kind as to enquire after M^r. John Lewis & [author's blank] Brooke two young Virginian Gent^n. lately arrived in New York from England—Their families are very Anxious to hear from them—If I sh^d. continue to forw^d. Flour or any other Articles for the use of our Prisoners, I could wish some settled Mode could be established for the Sloop going into New York without sending in for Passports on every different Occasion, as it would save Time & Trouble—If any other Article besides flour would answer better pray advise me of it—You will be pleased to discharge the Sloop as soon as possible, as it will

lessen the Charge—When I last heard from Home the Family were all well—We should be glad of a Line from our Long Island Friends, if it was only to know they were all well, and it the Letters were left open for the Examination of the proper Officer with you, they might be sealed & directed to me—I shall go home to morrow—

Am &

To William Atlee

Sir   Philadelphia Aug 11th. 1777

I received your favour, and am much obliged by your care and Attention in paying out the Monies forwarded for the British prisoners—I think it absolutely necessary to appoint a deputy Commissary of prisoners for your Quarter, as the service will require that Lancaster & Reading be made places of Confinement for such as shall be taken in this division of the states—It is necessary that this Appointment be made of a person of Abilities & Address as he will have to deal with a set of supercilious & haughty People—

The pay will be that of a Major and the same Rations—permit me, Sir, to make you an offer of the Department, as I know of none, whose character will better justify the nomination and do more service to the publick—

As the distance is great and delay dangerous, I have ventured to enclose the Appointment, which I hope you will accept; but if you should determine otherwise, I must beg the favour of you to execute it, untill I can be informed of your refusal and forward some other person to take the charge—The Enemy's fleet have again appeared, and make a show as if going up Chesopeak Bay—if so that may make an Attempt to deliver the prisoners with you—You will therefore, on the first intelligence of the fleets advancing towards the Head of the Bay, remove all the prisoners with you to the Town of Reading, and those at Reading, to Easton on the Delaware, taking new paroles from the Officers for the place where removed to—

I enclose you an Order of the Executive Council for a sufficient Guard—I also enclose a Copy of a Letter from the Officers at Reading, in which you can do as you think prudent—I would have them used with decency, if their Behaviour merit it, but by no means allowed to go about in the Night—I know Foster & Wilson of the 55th—they behaved exceedinly ill in New Jersey, especially Foster, and scarcely deserve the treatment due to Gentlemen—I am sorry to have Occasion to Say so much of prisoners—Our prisoners in New York are treated with great cruelty—Those on Long Island are on parole but are left to the Mercy of the Inhabitants, as no provision is made for their support—I shall be obliged to you to let one Alexander McNab of the 40th Reg^t. go to Easton in company with any proper person going that way, who will see him delivered to Robert L. Hooper Esqr. of that place, giving McNab a pass certifying his being exchanged for Robert Nugent of Col^o. Miles's Battalion, and desiring M^r. Hooper to let him go the shortest way to Amboy, writing to the commanding officer there, to send him over with a flag to Staten Island & taking a Rec^t. for him in Exchange for s^d. Robert Nugent who has arrived in this city, desiring the s^d. command^g officer to transmit the Rec^t. to me at HQ^{rs}.—McNab must draw provision of M^r Fr[anck]s Comm^y. at Lancaster for the journey—

Be so good as to let me have your answer directed to Head Quarters as soon as possible—

I had forgot to mention, that I had appointed Col^o. Haller in the Town of Reading to take the Direction of the Prisoners there, and and engaged to pay him for his trouble, I have never heard from him whether he would undertake the Trust or not—I must beg you will treat the matter with him with proper delicacy, as he may be of service to you, in continuing the oversight of them for which he shall be amply rewarded, it not being worth while to have a Commissary there for so few Prisoners

Enclosed—Commission dated 9th. Aug^t.—letter from Officers at Reading—Extract from Board of War ab^t Treatment of Prisoners— Order of Executive Council of Penn^{sa}. For a Guard—

Atlee, at Lancaster, Pennsylvania, accepted the position of Deputy Commissary General of Prisoners for that town and its environs.

Philadelphia 6 Augt. 1777 Gave Danl. Clymer Esqr. an appointment of Deputy Commissary of Prisoners in the usual form for Philadelphia

This notation occurs without any correspondence to Clymer.

To Samuel Miles

Camp at Warminster Township [Bucks County, Pa.]

Sir Augt. 14 1777

I doubt not but you have heard of the Success of the Motion made in Congress for leaving the Exchange of Prisoners entirely to his Exc^y the Commander in Chief—He has been pleased to authorized me to proceed in the Business, whenever an Opportunity shall offer—As the proposals from Genl. Howe were made thro' you, I have mentioned to his Exc^y. the Propriety of your going into the Enemy, in order to set this matter in a proper Channel—The General approves of the Measure, and has ordered me to write to you on the Subject. As I know you have this Exchange much at Heart, I doubt not but you will do every thing in your Power to expedite it, in which I shall most heartily join

Am Sir &c

Miles, Colonel of the Pennsylvania Rifle Regiment, had been taken prisoner on Long Island in August 1776. He was then on parole in Philadelphia.

To Joshua Mersereau

Sir Camp at Warminster, Bucks County [Pa.] Augt 14 1777

I have just rec^d. your several Letters of the 19th & 20th Ultmo and shall take Care to forward the enclosed—I am glad you have had the Pleasure of conducting General Prescott to his Quarters as I am sure he was properly treated—I have consulted the General on your Letter and would have you treat him with the greatest Politeness consistant with the securing him beyond a possibility of Escape I hardly think 12 Men a sufficient Guard—Let the Officer of the Guard have positive Orders to the above Effect.—The General may be indulged to walk out by Day with the Officer of the Guard, on his giving his Honor to take no improper advantage of the liberty so allowed him—You may also admit him to send in by a flag for any necessaries he may want from New Port, or to purchase them of the Inhabitants—From Genl. Howe's Conduct, there is but little hopes of a speedy Exchange for him, as the demand has been made 4 weeks ago & no answer returned—You may admit Lieu^t. Barrington to his Parole, to remain at some proper Place at a convenient distance from Genl. Prescott, but by no means to remain with him or in his Neighbourhood. The usual distance allowed to Officers on their Parole, is one Mile from their Lodging—As to News here we have none, except that we cannot find Genl. Howe—He has been embarqued 6 weeks—He appeared with his fleet off the Capes & remained there a few days, then disappeared 9 Days, and appeared again for three Days and has again disappeared and we know not what has become of him—We are waiting here, the Issue of these Manuvres—The weather is Hot to an extreme, how an Army on board Ship must beat it, I cannot say—Our News from the Northward is not so agreeable as I could wish, but not so bad as generally believed—It is the general Opinion that if the Eastern Militia turn out with Spirit, Mr Burgoyne is inevitably ruined—We are about to settle a general Exchange of all Officers but the two Generals. Therefore those Gentlemen you mention had better remain for a few days longer—I must beg you will consult with the Governor on some proper Measures for regulating the Prisoners so as to prevent the ill consequences you mention—

I cannot see M^r. Phonix & therefore beg you will secure the Sugar if possible & Rum if it be good—Sugar has got up here to £35 & Rum to 50/—you may about these having 1/6 as you please

There is no News from France by fair Promises.—Pray forward the Barracks as fast as possible, and let them be well calculated for the Purposes; including a good Room for the Commissary if he should choose to lodge there—

Am &c

To John Adam

Sir,   Camp Bucks County [Pa.] Augt. 14 1777

I duly rec^d your two last Letters, and am very sorry that the Enemy throw every Obstacle in their Power, in the way of helping our unhappy Prisoners—I yet hope you have rec^d Pasports for the Sloop, if not she must be unloaded for the use of the Army with you—I could wish Genl. Putnam would send in for an Answer one way or the other—At all Events send in the Letter to M^r. Pintard—We have no News here, not being able to tell what has become of Genl. Howe & his fleet—he appeared off [sic] last Thursday Friday & Saturday but has disappeared—Am &

To Richard Peters

Sir   Camp Bucks County [Pa.] Augt. 15th 1777
    The Bearer M^r. Joshua Messereau deputy Commissary of
Prisoners, has just returned from Massachusetts Bay whether I had
sent him to collect together & take charge of the Prisoners of War in
that & the neighboring States, supposing that the Barracks were in
forwardness for receiving them—The Accounts he gives me of the
State of the Prisoners there, and that the Barracks are not yet begun,
induces me to send him on to your City that he may personally give the
Board the same information he has done to me, whereby I doubt not
they will see a propriety in giving some further Orders about this
matter in order to have the Business speedily accomplished—He gives
a very bad Account of the situation chosen for the Barracks, and is of
opinion that the Building will be far more costly than on Connecticut
River and the annual Expence greatly encreased from the difficult Land
Carriage—However the Board will judge for themselves on hearing
the Circumstances from M^r. Messereau—I can recommend him as a
man of undoubted Probity & understanding in these matters, and who
deserves as much from the Publick for past Services as any Man of his
Standing whatever—
    Am &

To Lewis Pintard

Dr Sir   Camp in Bucks County [Pa.] Augt. 16 1777
    My last to you was from Peakskill, with a Sloop load of flour for
Sale on Acc^t. of our Prisoners with you—but am sorry to be informed
that no Answer has been yet given to the glad sent in to Kingsbridge
for proper passports for the same—As this mode of supplying our
Prisoners was proposed by M^r. Loring thro' you, I cannot account for
this conduct—I send enclosed the 1st. Bills of three Setts drawn in
your favour by David Franks on Nesbett D[rum]mond & Franks for
£200 Sterl. each on the whole acc^t. £600 Sterl. which I hope you will
immediately negotiate without any farther difficulty and distribute the
proceeds among our Prisoners for their immediate relief—Proper Care
will be taken to settle & discharge their Board due, which ought not to
be done out of this scanty supply, especially as it is largely in Advance

for the British Officers that have been & are Prisoners with us.—I also send herewith the following Sums—for L^t. W^m. Crawford four half Joh's—L^t. John Crawford Eight Half Johs, two Guineas, 1 dollar & one English Shilling—L^t. W^m. M^{ac}Pherson Seven half Johs—L^t: Joel Wertreat, three half Johs. & three Guineas—Lieu^t. Peter Meddagh Six half Johs—L^t. Joseph Martin three half Johs—L^t. John Randolph Six half Johs—Major W^m. Baily Eighty Nine Dollars—In the whole thirty Seven half Johs.—five Guineas Ninety Dollars & one English Shilling all which you will be pleased to deliver accordingly—I wish you would make application to the proper Officer concerning Passports for Provisions being sent in, if there have not arisen any Objections to the Measure—

I also enclose Captain Flahaven's Commission in Case it may be of any Service to him, it not being discovered till lately that he had it not with him—I lately sent in to your Care 100 Suits of Cloaths 200 Shirts & 200 p Shoes via Staten Island, which I hope are properly distributed—

Am &

P. S. I also send in for Ensign Saml Chickley £11: 3: 4 ½ Sterl. being 1 DbleLoon—two half Jos. Twelve Dollars, 15 Pistareens—5 quarter dollars 7 English Shillings—8 Shilling pieces & [   ] 6^d.—My Friend M^{rs}. Eliz: Ferguson has reason to believe that there are Letters in New York, from her Husband in Scotland, I must beg the fav^r. of you to enquire for them and if necessary put an Advertisement in the paper desiring they may be delivered to you for forwarding, if they can be admitted—I wrote you in my last begging you to endeavour to forward if permission could be obtained a few little Trifles presented to Miss Ricketts by her Brother in England, which are in the Hands of M^r. Peter Livingston, they can be directed to M^r. Chandler. M^{rs}. Anthony Stocker begs the same favour of you, as for M^{rs}. Ferguson— The wife of a Charles Hughs a Swiss, is said to be on Board the Preston Man of War, begs to know his Situation whether a Prisoner or Whether sent & how he does—She is much distressed and this would be but an Act of humanity—I also send 2 ½ Johs two half Guineas—2 3/8 Dollars for Lieu^t. John Woodside—

To Lewis Pintard

D^r. Sir   Elizabeth Town [N.J.] Augt. 26th 1777

By order of his Excellency the Commander in chief, I am arrived at this Town in order to wait an answer to the following Letter on business of importance to the Prisoners on each side of the Question—You may remember that you informed me sometime past that you were instructed to acquaint me that Genl. Howe would permit the sending in, any Quantity of Provision to the City of New York, to be sold for the Benefit of our unhappy Prisoners with you—This was confirmed be a letter from Mr Commissary Loring, to the same purpose—As soon as authorized by Congress, I repaired to the North river, where flour is most easily to be obtained at this season of the Year, loaded a Schooner with several hundred Barrels, and sent it to the out posts of the Enemy to obtain Passports for the Vessel proceeding to your City—this is upwards of three weeks ago and have not received an answer to this request, founded on the above assurance from & in the Name of Genl. Howe, which must undoubtedly give me the Priviledge to ask it now as a matter of right—As our Prisoners must Continue to Suffer unless Something is speedily done for them, I am to desire of you immediately on rec^t. of this to wait upon the Commanding Officer at New York and lay this matter before him, and ask Passports for any Quantity of flour that may be necessarily to Genl. Howes proposal—I should be glad (if not thought improper) to have liberty of sending it in both from the North & Rariton River, as at this season of the year, it is not easy to be obtained but at a distance in the Country which will make the land Carriage very inconvenient unless we can have some advantage from the water—I must beg the favor of you to let me hear from you tomorrow, as I shall wait the Evening here for that purpose. If any thing should obstruct the making out the Passports immediately, you can let me know if they can be sent, by the next opportunity, and I will in the mean time be collecting the flour together—

I enclose a second Letter of Bills of exchange on Nesbit Drummer &c for £600 Ster. in you favour, for the use of our Prisoners, having sent the first in my last—Enclosed you also have a letter & half Joh. for Henry Bedginer—five half Johs for Lieut^s. Turnbull & Furguson—half Joe & Moidore [sic] for [writer's blank] a Guinea & twelve Dollars for Philip Fulkerson—

I shall write to M^r. Fells family & see that a proper remittance is made to him without delay—

    Am &

PS, It is reported at Head Quarters that a Captain Travern now a Prisoner in your Provost Guard, is treated in the most harsh & Cruel Manner—If this is not true, I would wish that Captain Travern would write me a line on the subject as it may prevent some disagreeable consequences—

A moidore was a Portuguese coin, then in common use.

To John Campbell

Sir   Eliz. Town [N.J.] Augt 27th. 1777

    I lately sent Mr Joshua Mercerau Deputy Comy of Prisoners with a Number of your maimed Prisoners from the City of Philadelphia, who earnestly petitioned to be returned to you in order to be properly provided for, with orders to deliver them under the Sanction of a flag of Truce, to the Commanding Officer of the British Troops on Staten Island—as it is a matter of consequence to both Armies that proper decency should be observed towards flaggs of Truce who come duly authorised and on Business of importance, I cannot but enclose you a Copy of Mr Merceraus letter to me on my arrival in this Town, on which I will only observe that his treatment was a very dishonorable, mean & unwarrantable return for a Journey of almost 100 Miles on the sole purpose of conveying those poor Fellows to their own People agreeable to their request—

    on my arrival here last night, I found a Number of the Inhabitants of Staten Island made Prisoners by Genl Sullivans division a few days past: as these People are now under my Care, I think proper to let you know that I am ready to exchange them for an equal Number of our Inhabitants who may be Prisoners with you provided I can have an answer before I leave this Town, which will be tomorrow Evening or the next morning very early—

I would take it as a particular favor if the Bearer might be permitted to go over to New York with the enclosed letter, as I am very anxious to have an immediate answer; he is one of the Inhabitants above referred to, who has earnestly desired to be sent over that he might solicit an

Exchange for himself & Neighbours If he is not admitted to go to New York, I will be much obliged by your forwarding the letter to M^r. Pintard immediately on receipt—
I have the honor to be &

Campbell was a British Brigadier General commanding on Staten Island.

To John Campbell

Sir E. T. Ferry [Elizabethtown, N.J.] Augt. 28 1777
your favor by Major Courtland have just been delivered in answer to which can assure you that Mr Mercereau was sent by me from the Camp near Philadelphia with your Maimed Soldiers, being the only Deputy Commissary of Prisoners I then had with me, and his being a native of Staten Island, was altogether an adventitious Circumstance, and which was not adverted to when he was Sent, especially as it was uncertain wether he would go to Powles Hook or Staten Island—
I doubt not that your Sentiments of this subject being made known to the Troops under your command, and will prevent any future dissatisfaction—your Sentiments relative to taking the Innocent Inhabitants agree with my own and those of most of the Officers of the American Army, and verily believe had not Coll. Dungan set the Example on his late Visit to Woodbridge, the Inhabitants of Staten Island had remained in safety—However sir in confidence that the principles suggested in your letter will be carried into execution and the Inhabitants from Woodbridge &c returned to their habitations in peace, I return with Major Courtland, 24 of the Inhabitants of your Island taken by Genl Sullivans Division—
I am &

To Lewis Pintard

Camp Pensylvania [Pennypackers Mills, Pa.]
D^r. Sir Sep^t 28th 1777
An Opportunity offering this Moment, I can only delay so long as to send you for the use of some of our Prisoners, the following Sums of Money, for Lieu^t. James M^c.farlane 2 ½ Guineas & 4 Joes—for Lieu^t John Holiday 2 half Jos. 3 Guineas & one Moidore—for Lt Obadeel

M^c.Leen one half Joe 1½ Dollar for L^t. Robert Campbell Ten half Joes, for Capt. Thomas Campbell 98 English shillings one Dollar one half Crown, I have also directed twenty half Joes to be sent with this from my house for the use of John fells Esqr. after deducting what may be necessary for any thing [he] had on my Acc^t.—I have lately received an Acc^t. from my Deputy in New England that the British Prisoners there were in great want of Cloathing a particular State of which shall write to Genl. Howe by the first flag—

To William Howe

His Excellency Genl. Sir William Howe

Sir   *at Skippack [Pa.] Sep^t. 30th 1777*
By letters late received from the Commissaries in New England, I am informed that your Prisoners in our hands are in great want of Cloaths, and as the weather in that Country will soon call for a supply, I take the Liberty to acquaint you with it in time, that proper provision may be made for them—
Did I know were to find M^r. David Franks, I should not have troubled your Excellency with this—
Have the Honor to be with due respect   Sir Your most Obe Hbl. Servant

Howe was Commander-in-Chief of the British Army in North America.

To Joshua Loring

Sir   Octr. 6th. 1777
By the return of the Prisoners Exchanged as inclosed in your last I find several of them are late Prisoners in Companion with a number yet in Captivity—The agreement made between Gen Howe & Genl. Washington was that exchanges in General should take place according to the time of Captivity—I have therefore to prevent Complaints return'd the Paroles & desire you will send out Officers in their paroles who were taken on Long Island last summer—Being at a distance from my Books & papers cannot mention them by Name except a Captain Van Dyke who I believe was one of the first Prisoners last summer—I wrote you some time since relative to

a Doctor Sandon who went to New York on his parole & desired that he might be accepted in exchange for Doc^t. M^c.Henry, to which I have not received your answer—You will please to enclose Doc^t McHenrys parole for Doc^t Sandon or any other Doct^r. that is with you under the like Circumstances—If this should take place, I do engage to send in Doctor Mengin as soon as he can had from the place of his residence, for Doc^r. Wiggins, agreeable to his Parole shewn to me by him—I lately rece^d. information from New England that the British Prisoners there are in the greatest want of Cloathing, which the weather will speedily call for a full supply of—

If you think a partial Exchange of the Prisoners now in Captivity without regard to the disputes existing between the respective Commanders in Chief, would be accomplished, I will do all in my power to forward it.—

To Timothy Pickering

D^r. Sir Baskenridge [N.J.] Octr. 19th. 1777

On my way from Camp I was taken with a very severe fever, & it was with difficulty I reached this place were I have been for some days confined to my Bed, but am now on the recovery.—I have been much elated with a report from the Northward, that Genl. Burgoine with his whole Army have surrendered Prisoners of War, I am too well acquainted with the practice of News manufacturing, to put entire Confidence in this report, but as I shall soon be able to proceed on the business I came about & as soon as finished shall immediately push for Camp. I thought it best to send the Bearer to Express to know what alteration the accounts from the Northward may occasion in my department—I must therefore beg the favor of you to let me know the Situation of affairs in that Quarter according to the last acc^{ts}. if there are any number of Prisoners taken, pray obtain such directions from the General as he may think necessary, especially as Massachusetts Bay & Connecticut are already so stocked with Prisoners; that it will be impossible to furnish a greater Number with Bread, without the enamoes Expence & also injuring our Northarn Army—If Genl. Burgoine or any other principle Officers should be Prisoners, I should be glad to know if the Genl. has any particular orders relative to the place of their destination & Paroles—On Wednesday last 14 Transports with the Foreign Troops on Board sailed from Staten Island where bound is not known

Altho' I am sensible of your constant hurry & the importance of every moment of your time, I must beg you will indulge me with an acc^t. of your present Situation & any remarkable occurance since I left you as I am exceedinly anxious for your welfare & Success—

By means of my Brother I have set a considerable number of Shoemakers at work, & hope to take with me on my return some evidence of their labour. Had attention been paid to this last spring many Thousands pairs of Shoes might have now been ready—

I have an offer from three Substantial Men immediately to erect a large Tannery in a secure place, That they will Tan from 1500 to 2000 Hides p^r Annum one half of the leather shall be the property of the Continent, which shall be all sold for shoes the other half (their property) shall be also sold for shoes, to be delivered at the Current price—if the Genl. will authorize me to enter into this agreement, I will do it before I return—

The Undertakers are to be at the whole expence & the Trouble of delivering the Shoes—but case of destruction by the Enemy the Continent to loose their part of the Leather destroyed as the Undertakers run the risque of the rest—

I am &

Pickering was the Adjutant General of Washington's army.

To Lewis Pintard

Dr Sir   Baskenridge [N.J.] Novem^r. 3^d. 1777

Having just got the better of my late Indisposition I went to Elizabeth Town where I found your Letter of the 25 Ultimo with the acc^t. Sales of 500 Bbls of Flour, and the expenditure of the neat Proceeds wereof all had given me the greatest Satisfaction—Had it not been for my illness, I would have sent in the flour mentioned in my last—With this you will receive a small boat Load as p^r invoice enclosed being the first part of 500 Barrels ready here for sending over and which the want of a proper Boat prevents all going together, but which will only cause a second Trip, The Boatmen is directed agreeable to your instruction to call on the Man of War at the Narrows, The great increase of the demand of flour occasioned by the addition of Genl. Burgoine's Army to the number of Prisoners with us has risen the price & caused a present scarcity this added to my being oblidged immediately to go to Congress, will prevent my sending in such a Quantity immediately as I intended, but as I shall leave orders for Collecting a proper Quantity in my absence, you may depend on it as soon as I return,—I shall vary the Cargoes & send in Wheat or Corn as I find it most Convenient & Profitable—In the meantime if you can get necessaries for our Prisoners on Credit or can ever borow a sum of money of interest for a Month or two I will carefully reimburse you—you may go as far as 500 Barrels more—if the Officers in the City choose to go to Long Island I must beg the favor of you to become answerable for their Board at 2 Dollars p^r week untill you hear again from me, as in the meantime I will get instructions from the Congress on this Head, I am sorry that this measure is necessary as we must proceed in the same line here, which must occasion very great distress to many of the Officers Prisoners with us, who already suffer for many necessaries notwithstanding what they have received from us. when you pay any thing for any Officer either in Board or otherwise let the officer Countersign the receipt—

The hurry of a Camp has prevented my acknowledging the Rec^t of the Bills of exchange first sent & returned by you—I also duly received the Officers rec^t for the amount of the bulls sent you which were drawn in you favor. The 3^d. Sett of which I now enclose—The Cloathing you receive in the Case marked stores 3^d. Pen^s. Reg^t. was sent in a mistake of the Officer at Eliz^n. Town but as the Cloaths will be useful with you I will settle the matter here—I received your note about the Women who wanted to go from Monmouth to New York, permission for which should have interested myself to obtain, but an act of our Assembly has lately passed as I am informed, giving such Persons liberty to sell their effects & go to New York, so that I suppose they will embrace the opportunity, you forgot to mention if you heard of the young Gent. Mentioned in one of my late letters which I should be glad to know—I must beg the favor of your to distribute among such Prisoners as are inhabitants of the state of New York & not Prisoners of war & who you think are in the greatest distress the sum of Ten Guineas & one shilling & take a seperate receipt for the same, also 29 2/3 Dollars amongst the most distressed of our Prisoners of War (privates) with also separate receipts these sums you may deduct out of the next proceeds of the flour, unless it will not be inconvenient to wait till the next parcel of flour sent in when I will send some Commodity for this purpose I send herewith for Henry Bedinger five ½ Joe & one Guinea—for John Reed three ½ Jos & for James Lingan Two half Jos &

five for Coll Allen in future after your letters to me are examined by a proper Officer, pray seal them at the distance they have to come to my hands under an open letter more apt to be lost—

 Am &

To Joshua Loring

Sir   Baskinridge [N.J.] Novem^r 3^d. 1777

 I wrote you Lately by Doct^r Wiggins from Camp in Pensylvania enclosing the parole sent out the 27 Sep^t. in order that they might be exchanged for those who were captivated before them I should not have given you this trouble but to prevent a jealousy that Prisoners are exchanged from favor without respect to their due order—I then had not my Books or papers with me, but on examination find that the following Pris. Officers have been long in Captivity, altho' I know not wether they are all with you or not as some of them were taken in Canada—Capt. Theodoris Bliss—Ebenezer Sullivan—John Stevens—Eben^r. Green— Vandyke—Wills—the following Lieut^s are also of those who were taken very early in 1776 Obadieh McCalester—John Green—Samuel McFarin— John Edie—& Henry T[reen]—& Thomas G[rover]—any of these Gen^t. if with you or on parole with us would be very acceptable in exchange merely because it will be in the order of their Captures—

Sometime since I returned a Number of Inhabitants taken from Staten Island by Genl Sullivan upon exchanging sentiments with Genl. Campbell on the subject, whereby I had reason to expect a return of the Inhabitants taken by Coll. Dungan in Woodbridge—I am informed that some of these are accordingly returned, but that six of them are yet detained Viz Benjamin Thonell Timothy Bloomfield—Jere. Clarkson—Walter Shurston—Martin & Stephen Combs—I suppose this to proceed from a mistake & doubt not the will be accordingly suffered to return—I have had application from several Cap[se] of your officers from different places, desiring me to acquaint you that they are in want of necessaries for the winter—Major Edmisten in particular informs & that those lately at Easton with him, were in want of shoes Stockings & shirts, which I suppose must be the case with the others, I am also informed that the Hessian Officers at Dumfries are in great want of money & the Privates in General want Cloaths—

As Business will necessarily arise wherever the scene of action is, I should be glad of knowing to whom I must direct as Commissary of Prisoners with the Army under Gen[l]. Howe

Early last spring I interested myself in gaining permission for Gambell of the 47 Commissary M[c]Cullogh & ensign Camp[bell] of the 15 to go into New York upon parole that they would send out proper Officers in Exchange & return forthwith Since their departure in March last have not heard from these Gentleman, but am yet without an exchange—

Having been detained from Camp by a slight indisposition Since I wrote you by Doc[t]. Wiggins, I know not wether he is returned or any answer given to the letter by him, & as Doc[t]. M[c].Henry is very pressing to know his fate, will be considered as exchanged for Doc[t]. Sandon unless you contradict it speedily—

To the Commissary of Prisoners in the British army in Philadelphia

Sir   Camp [White Marsh, Pa.] Novem[r] 12 1777

On a late Journey through New Jersey I called at the Hospital at Princeton to see the state of the Hessian Prisoners there—I found them in want of Cloaths &c to a very great degree—but as the enclosed letter from the Surgeon will explain their wants best—I refer you to it—I have repeatedly mentioned the necessity of making Provisions for winter Cloathing of the Prisoners, but have received no answer: if this is delayed they must inevitably suffer, as many of them are in Connecticut and about [8]00 in Dumfries & Winchester in Virginia—I am requested to beg to favor of your getting permission for the Baron de C[e]ntuacy a Volunteer in our Service and lately made a Prisoner by you, to come as far as the rising sun on friday morning next, when M[r] David Franks, I am informed will have a conference there, with one of his agents in presence of a British Officer—the design of the Barons attendance, is just to settle some little Business with Major Bladgon which may also be done in the presence of the British Officer—

I am instructed by his Excellency Gen[l]. Washington to inform you that he has rec[d] repeated complaints that our Prisoners with you are Suffering greatly for want of Provisions: as this would be a return, he could hardly expect from the full supply granted to your Prisoners on every occasion, he hopes the complaints are without foundation, but the true State of which he request you will furnish him with, as it is not his design that any of his Army should suffer tho' in Captivity—I should be much obliged to you for a list of the Prisoners with you, & will return the Compliment when you desire it—From the great number of Prisoners that have been sent to Massachusetts Bay for the more expiditious embarkation for Europe, it has become impossible to supply the whole with flour on so sudden a demand—I am very apprehensive that they will suffer greatly for want of this article, unless you can obtain me Passports for a Vessel to go from Maryland or Virginia to Boston with a load—I would if agreeable, also send a Vessel load to New York for the use of our Prisoners there—as the season of the Year advances, it requires that these Voyages be hastened as far as possible, must therefore beg as speedy an answer as in your Power—I should have made this application sooner, but have been long absent from Camp—

As I have been not yet informed what Gentleman fills the department of Commissary of Prisoners in Philidelphia, you will ensure the direction—

Am Sir

Sent with the above letter, to John Morris £6..19..6 to Christopher Meyers one half Joe—

28th. Octr. 1777 wrote to Isaac Zane, Wm Attlee, Wm Haller & Robt L. Hooper for return of all Prisoners under their Care on the 1st. Novr.

Sent Isaac Zane his Deputation for State of Virginia dated 6 Sept 1777

Sent Ezekiel Williams his Deputation for the State of Connecticut dated 14th. Novr. 1777

Sent Novr. 14 1777 Lt Woodson 2 ½ Jos 1 Guinea 8 Dollars Humphrey Bate 4 Dollars & Baggs of necessaries, Baggage of 9 Regiments

Boudinot's notations on letters that do not appear in this letterbook.

To Lewis Pintard

Dr Sir   Camp near Phila. [White Marsh, Pa.] Novemr. 18 1777

I arrived here on the 11th. after being Detained by the way sometime by a return of my fever, I hope you have received some part of the flour from Brunswick. I have this day wrote into Genl Howes Camp to obtain permission to send a Vessel load of flour to you from Maryland or Virginia, if this can be accomplished, it will save a great deal of trouble—I send herewith the following sums of money

for James Lingan   £32..8..00
Capt John Carlise   50..0..1
James Heron 7 ½ Jos   21..0..0
Lt John Gale 4 D^o 12..0..0
Robert Chesley 9 ½ Guineas

I hope to hear from you by the first opportunity of how our Friends on the Island are—love to all of them—

And am D^r sir Yours very aff.

To Robert Lettis Hooper

D^r. Sir   Camp Whitemarsh [Pa.] Novr. 13th. 1777

Having the misfortune of a relapse of my fever on my way to Camp, has occasioned the delay of an answer to yours of 2^d. Inst^t.—The Prisoners you mention ought to be added to the general Return, but for this purpose it is necessary that I should have their Names, Corps, time when & Place where taken, which I must beg as soon as possible; if an Opportunity first offers to Reading send it there to the Care of Coll. Haller, as I expect to set off for York Town some time next Week—I enclose you a Letter for Mr Duyckink, ag^t. whom great Complaints are made from your Town, which has almost staggered me with regard to his releasement—However if we Err let us do it on the side of Mercy—I must therefore beg you will take his Parole in the Strongest Terms, to continue at his farm and within two Miles thereof &c &c &c To this must be added a Bond from two Securities in £1000—Conditioned for his observing the Parole & his good Behaviour—This is a precaution necessary to justify me, and can be no hardship to him—You will enclose me these Papers when he is discharged—I expected e'er this to have had some directions about Major Edminston, but as I have not yet received any, I think he had best go on with the first Opportunity for York Town, where I hope to meet him and if he is to be exchanged, will prevent his going farther if not, he will be so far on his way to Virginia—As I expect to set off about the middle of next week, I think he had best set off sooner—I enclose a Letter to him—

The Pay & Rations of all my Deputies are that of a Major—you may depend on my best Endeavours in fav^r of Mr Byles—

Am &c

To John Duyckinck

Sir   Camp [White Marsh, Pa.] Novr. 13 1777

The Various Complaints ag^t. you from Easton has rendered your liberation more difficult then I had imagined, however I have determined to confide in your Integrity, especially as you must by this Time know by Experience the disadvantages that will arise from a Contrary Conduct—for my Justification I have added to your Parole, a Bond & Security mentioned in a Letter to M^r. Hooper—This can be no disadvantage to you, and may Show my attention to every Term that the publick could reasonably expect—

I also enclose a late resolution of Congress necessary for you to know in particular, as every one will be watching your Conduct—

M^r. Hooper will release you to return to your House & to remain there & within two Miles of it—It gives me Pleasure when in my Power to relieve or alleviate the distresses of my fellow Creatures in whatever Circumstances, and I hope in this Instance I shall have no reason to repent this Indulgence—

Am &

John Duyckinck of New Jersey had been a Colonel in the New Jersey Militia, but was reported as a British sympathizer. He would not take the loyalty oath under Washington's proclamation, and in early 1777 Washington ordered him confined as too "dangerous" to be at liberty. At this time he was being held at Easton, Pa.

To Charles Edmonstone

Sir   Camp [White Marsh, Pa.] Novr. 13 1777

Some time since I rec^d. a Letter from you relative to the distresses of the English Prisoners at Easton, and desiring liberty to send an Officer to New York to get the necessary relief for them—Altho' my Indisposition prevented my answering your Letter, yet I had an Opportunity of sending an Acc^t. thereof to M^r. Loring in New York. I had previous to this wrote to New York on this Subject, but have never rec^d any Answer—As to the Liberty of sending an Officer into New York for this Purpose, it is out of my Power to gratify you, but whatever necessaries are sent out for the Prisoners, shall be carefully forwarded to any Person appointed by your Commissary to receive & distribute the same, in like manner as Mr Pintard is allowed to proceed in New York. Your last letter of 7th. Octr. was

delivered to me not till yesterday
  Am Sir Yours &

Edmonstone was Major of the British Eighteenth Regiment of Foot.

To Abraham B. Bancker

Sir   Camp [White Marsh, Pa.] Novr. 13 1777
  M^r. Peters put into my Hands a Letter from you mentioning your
Appointment as Com: of Pris. for New York in Consequence of a resolve
of Congress—Since that period, the Power of appointing Commissaries in
the different States is vested solely in me, and had not this Office been
filled up by the Appointment of Mr John Adam who has resided at
Peakskill all Summer, I should with Pleasure have complied with the
Recommendation of the Councill of Safety of your State, by giving you
that Office—
  Am &c

Bancker had been an officer in the Fourth New York Regiment. The *Journals of the
Continental Congress* do not show he was given the appointment referred to.

To William Atlee

Sir,   Camp Whitemarsh [Pa.] Novr 13 1777
  Your favour of the 23^d Ultmo has lately come to hand, having been
absent from Camp some time by a slight Indisposition—Whatever
Services I can possibly render to your Brother you may depend upon will
be done with very great Pleasure—
  I am sorry to say that every obstacle that can be [ ]nd by Genl Howe
is thrown in the Way to prevent an Exchange while at the same time he is
suggesting to out Prisoners that it is all General Washington's fault—one
of our Officer Prisoners in Phil: lately wrote out that he was authorized to
acquaint Gen. Washington that Genl. Howe was ready to Exchange the
whole of the Prisoners on the easiest Terms, not regarding the dispute
between them ab^t. the dead Prisoners—Genl. Washington immediately
accepted the Proposal when Genl. Howe made the Compliance with this
old demand a point to be complied with previous to any Exchange—
There is no dependance on any Proposals made by the Bye, so that I am

afraid an Exchange is not so near as we imagined—I am sorry for any unnecessary Trouble you have with the Prisoners, and really think the Board of War should be carefull of the orders they issue, as they often cause difficulties that they little think of—Hope to see you in a few Days in the mean Time

Am Dr Sir &

To Joshua Mersereau

D^r. Sir,   Camp Whitemarsh [Pa.] Novr 13 1777

By means of severe Indermitting fever, which has confined me sometime, I have been prevented writing you for some time, but am again returned to Camp.—The glorious News from the Northward has greatly raised our Spirits, and indeed is one of those kind interpositions of an overruling Providence, that we ought never to forget—Few know the Consequences that would have followed in Gen Gates's defeat—I know not but it might have proved fatal to us—This raises the advantages of this Victory beyond the base overcoming the English Army—But now they are conquered & Prisoners what are you to do with them—How are you to supply them with Provisions—You must exert every Nerve & get such assistance as is in your Power—In order to aid you I have sent in to Genl. Howe for Passports for a Vessel load of flour to go to your from Maryland—I hope he will grant it, if he does not be the blame upon him, we can do no more—

You must be exceeding Carefull to take the most exact lists of all the Prisoners of Gen. Burgoynes Army—Their Names, Corps, Size, Age, Country, Trade &c &c These lists must be forwarded to me as Returns— A Book must be made to Contain the Parole of these Prisoners & they must sign in the same order as they are set down in the lists—The Officers must also sign their Paroles separately—You must employ a Clerk for the Time being & Consult the General on the Propriety & regularity of what you think necessary to be done—

I must beg you will immediately make out returns of all Prisoners under your Care on the first day of this Ins^t. & transmit them to me immediately—

I wish you would finished the Matter with M^r. Dean and what ever is to be forwarded, send to my House at Baskinridge—

We have the most shocking Acc^ts. here of your Extravagancies in the Prices of every Article—What is to become of us, I know not, unless some immediate Stop can be put to this abominable Extortion—They have began in this State & I hope will proceed.

No News stirring, except the Success of Capt Weeks & others having taken 52 East Indiamen in the Channel, and that L^d. Stormont is recalled from the Court of France—

Enclosed is the Letter to the President from the Board of War—

Captain Weeks was Lambert Wickes of the Continental Navy.

To John Adam

Sir   Camp Whitemarsh [Pa.] Novr 13 1777

Your favour of the 4th. Inst^t. is now before me, I have just got to Camp from my late illness, and am exceedingly rejoiced to hear of the glorious Success of our northern Army—Your Letters of the 24th. & 30th. Ultmo with the returns, have not yet got to hand, I cannot conceive what has become of them—I must beg the favour of your making an exact return of all the Prisoners you have with you on the first of this Inst^t. as I am making out general returns for Congress as of that day—I have been informed that there are a number of Prisoners of War at Goshen; how came they there pray enquire & dispose of them properly making return &c

Be so kind as to furnish me with your News Papers as often as Convenient, as every thing of that kind is entertaining in a Camp—

No News stirring here except Capt. Weeks having taken (in Co. with some other Privateers) 52 West Indiamen in the Channell & Lord Stormont is called home—

Am &

To Elbridge Gerry

D^r. Sir   Camp Whitemarsh [Pa.] Novr. 13th 1777

Your favour of the 10th. Ultmo has just got to hand, and observe the Contents relative to Mess^s. Willson & McDonald—I am sorry to say that you have been in some measure misinformed with regard to M^r. Willson—He was taken at Somerset in N Jersey with a M^r. Foster, who tho' treated in the politest manner by Genl. Washington behaved so as to give general

Offence where they were quartered—On this I sent them to Philadelphia where they behaved with great Insolence to Genl. Gates—After they left Philadelphia & went to Lancaster I had frequent Complaints of their ill Behaviour—indeed all agreed that Foster was the principal agressor & was the means of Willson's bad Conduct—We are now negotiating a general Exchange, which I would hope might be accomplished if the most ungenerous Acts were not used to prevent it, and at the same time to Cast the Blame on Us—Circumstances are such at Present that it would not be consistent with the good of the Service to suffer an Officer to go in & return again, but as soon as it can be done with Propriety, your recommendation shall be attended to with great Pleasure—I expect soon to be at York where I shall have an opportunity of conversing further with you on this Head

Have the honor to be with great respect

Gerry was a Delegate to Congress which was then meeting at York, Pa.

To Richard Peters

Dr Sir   Camp [Pa.] Novr. 13 1777

On my Arrival in Camp, being absent some time past by severe Indisposition, your favours of [author's blank] Ins^t. was delivered me—I should have immediately attended the Board of War, but the Genl. has detained me a few days till a matter of some Importance relative to the Exchange of Prisoners is settled between his Exc^y & Genl Howe—As soon as this is done shall set off for York—

Am &

To Joshua Mersereau

D^r. Sir   Camp Whitemarsh [Pa.] Novr 14 1777

I wrote you yesterday, since which I have rec^d yours of the 4th. Inst^t. with the Bundle from Massachusets Bay and other Letters by Express—You must well remember the Treatment I rec^d. from the Board of War relative to the Barracks, I was therefore determined not to trouble myself farther about them, but as the necessity of Affairs have so increased & the public Good requires it, I intend to lay the Matter before the Congress, whether I am going in a few days, when I will immediately let you know the result, in the mean Time, you can go no farther than hiring either House or Vessel on the most reasonable Terms in your Power, and should be exceedingly glad you would get the Approbation of the Gov[r] and Councill to any Contract you may make—I must beg you will not let out any Prisoners to labour, that you can possibly find Places to Confine, as they greatly taint the Minds of the People, get a Knowledge of the Country and have an Opportunity of deserting & by which means we have lost many, while our poor fellows are kept in the closest manner with scarce the necessaries of Life—I must repeat my request for an exact return of all Prisoners under your Care, especially in Massct. Bay on the first day of Nov[r] Inst[t]. with the usual particulars—You must get assistance as you want it allowing a reasonable Price for the Time they are engaged—the less you can make out with the better, as the Expences run high—The Enemy raise every Objection to a general Exchange in their Power, and no particular one can be allowed but in the order of Capture—If any Person you deal with insists upon hard money (unless it is from an Officer Prisoner with us.) you are to report in to the Gov[r]. & Councill—Suffer no Officer to send for Paper Money & stop all you meet with & lay it before the Gov[r] & Councill, assigning the reason that our Papper is Counterfeited in New York & publickly advertised for Sale—Besides they first rob us of that which is good, sell it for 10 pC[t]: and then pay it to us in full Tale—As to the Waggons, if you want them you must certainly keep them at the Price given here by the Quarter Master, unless they can be had cheaper in your Country, and you must employ People to assist you as Commissary to provide for the Prisoners—

Nothing was done to purpose here after you left us, except the Battle of German Town, a particular Acc[t]. I sent to M[r]. Broome which you have undoubtedly seen—I am distressed to see your Papers filled with such horrid falsehoods relative to our Transactions here; scarcely an Article that has the most distant foundation in Truth—This must expose us greatly to the ridicule of the Enemy—I think your Papers are at least Equal to Gaine & Rivington—The extreme illusage given to many of our Gentlemen by your Printers, in inserting their Names to Letters wrote in a hurry for private inspection, makes those of Character afraid of giving you any Intelligence at all—

Since the Battle of German Town, an Attempt was made by about 2000 Hessians under Count Donop to storm fort Mercer at red Bank—They expected no Opposition—The Commanding Officer had contracted the works, removing the Cannon from the outer to the inner Work—The

Enemy came up in two Columns, and some of that had gained the outer Work, was huzzaing on the Day being their own when they rec^d such a Salutation as put them into the utmost confusion—The Contest lasted but 17 Minutes, when they retreated with the utmost precipitation—Our Garrison were so small that they did not dare to pursue, otherwise few would have returned to tell their Misfortune—They acknowledge the Loss to be 372, some think it greater—Count Donop is Dead, and greatly lamented his having entered the Service—spoke highly of the Generosity of his Treatment, he having threatned to put all to the Sword, had he succeeded—There have been also to Vessels blown up in the River, the Augusta of 64 Guns & Merlin of 22 Guns—They are almost continually harassing those brave Garrisons & Crews night & Day with a heavy Cannonade—They stand it out with a resolution that would do honor to the oldest Troops in Europe—They have not only the Ships of War to deal with, but five bomb Batteries from the Province Island—They have lost but few men among which is Capt. Treat of the Artillery a very brave & resolute Officer who has gained great Applause—We also have taken many straggling Parties & posts of Picketts of both Horse & foot, from Time to Time, indeed they very seldom peep beyond their Lines, close into the City—They have no Provisions but what they run up the River from their Shipping—We lately took 60 Prisoners at once from off Province Island—

I wish you to forward the Certificates of Mess^s. Deane & Webb as soon as possible—I shall give orders at Baskinridge for the reception of your Waggons—Let me know if I am to call on Mr Phonix for any more, and how much—I should be glad if you would write to a M^r. Paulding at Peeks kill & get him to send by your Waggons a Barrell of Salmon left there for me by Mr Jerem. Wadsworth, as he sent it forward & it has never come to hand but suppose it to be at his House—Lest I should not get that I wish you could forward me one, of any sort of Salt Fish—

I am so extremely hurried that I must omit more particular Instructions at this Time, as I have scarce Time to eat—

To Ezekiel Williams

Sir   Camp Whitemarsh [Pa.] Novr. 14th 1777
Your favour of the 7th. Ins^t. has just been handed to me—I am so exceedingly hurried at present, that I am obliged to defer particular

Instructions to you, but enclose your Deputation [alone] especially as on my return from Congress whether I am going in a few days I shall be able to give you them more full & certain—I doubt not from your Experience in this Business and your general Character, that you will be able to get the Affairs of this department in that regularity & order that will do your Credit—Let all the Acc^ts. from the 12th Aprill last be separated from those previous to that Day—No News stirring here, except that Capt. Weeks & others have taken 52 Sail of west indiamen & that Lord Stormont is recalled from Paris—we have daily Skirmishing & have taken several Prisoners lately—Our little Garrisons down the River make a most glorious resistance altho' continually harassed with a heavy Cannonade from Land & water—

Be so kind as to forward me without delay a full return of the Prisoners with you on the first Ins^t. with the usual Particulars—

Williams at Wethersfield, Connecticut, was Deputy Commissary General of Prisoners for that state.

To Joshua Loring

Sir   Camp Pennsylv. [White Marsh, Pa.] Novr. 24 1777

Yours of the 15th. Inst^t. I rec^d. yesterday, but have not seen the one referred to in it—I enclose your Exchange of 27 Sepr. and also one I had drawn up previously to the rec^t of yours, which I hope will have no objection too, or at least will approve of something very like it—I find all the Gent^n. mentioned therein unaccounted for and therefore am desirous t[hat] those of our Officers longest in Captivity may have their Exchange perfected.

I have examined the lists of Prisoners of War but cannot find any one of the Name of D^r. Church & know of none in Boston Goal, but our former director Genl. of the Hospital who was confined for some Mal Practice, and is a State Prisoner, being an Officer under us, and never in the King of Englands Service since this dispute, which makes me conclude there must be some Mistake in your Information—I am therefore in hopes D^r M^acHenry may be properly taken in the Exchange—The Prisoners taken with Gen. Burgoyne must inevitably suffer at Boston for want of flour if I am not permitted to send it from Virginia or Maryland—I have wrote in to Philadelphia on this Head, but cannot get an Answer—I intended also to send a Load to New York for our Prisoners there, which would save delay & Trouble—The State of the Prisoners on both Sides, gives me a great uneasiness—If you mean by general Exchange, one to be agreed to by us, without respect to the dispute subsisting between our two Generals, I will endeavour to accomplish it without delay—I am of opinion that could we meet on this Business, the whole might be easily settled on rational Terms, but at all events, I could wish all the Prisoners might be released before Winter, either on Parole or Exchanged Man for Man & Officer for Officer—The Hessians lately taken at red Bank &c are almost naked as well as many of the British Troops & must suffer if the Season sets in as usual—I have mentioned this matter in strong Terms by a Letter sent into Philadelphia, but have not rec^d any Answer—

Beside the Officers mentioned in the return enclosed, I also send a list of a number I find stand in my Books as unexchanged tho' sent in, but as they went in before my Appointment, I must beg the favour of your letting me know if they have been Exch^d. & for whom & if not to add them to the return—

To Lewis Pintard

Dr Sir   Camp Pennsylv. [White Marsh, Pa.] Novr. 24 1777
I have just rec^d your favour of the 15th Inst; and in Answer to your Enquiry about the Sailors, at Present I cannot direct the Cloathing of any but those taken in Continental Vessels of War, but will get an order to reach them all if possible, as soon as I get to Congress. I have not rec^d any Answer to my request for Passports to send flour from Maryland to your City—If this could be done, one Load would answer your whole present demands, which I am yet in hopes to accomplish—

I rec^d. a Letter from M^r. Cochran & would comply with his request but believe he has been misinformed with regard to the Laws of the State of Jersey, as they allow of no such Latitude, but whatever I can do, shall be done—I am surprized he does not send for the Children to L. Island as they are not in any way of gaining any thing where they are, but must be ruined—

I Enclose 3 ½ Jos. & 2 Dollars for Elihu Hall Lieu^t taken on Staten Island—

To Robert MacKenzie

Sir   Camp [White Marsh, Pa.] Novr. 25 1777

By direction from Joshua Loring Esqr I trouble you with the enclosed Letters, together with several Sums of money and a few Cloaths for our Prisoners, all contained in a pair of Saddlebags—To save you Trouble, if they were delivered to Major Joyns of the 9th Virg. Reg^t, he would see them properly distributed—I add at foot a list of the Monies and for whom—

Am Sir &

9th. Virg Reg^t

Cap Geo. Gilchrist & Ensign Stockley	£20 00
Saml Weples	35 Dollars
Cap & Lieut Snead	10-0-0 Virginia
Ensign N. Darby	19.6.3
Lieut. Sev. Teckle	6.13.6
L^t. Thos. Parker	12
L^t. Thos. Custis	9-11
Major Joyns	10-17-6-

MacKenzie, a Captain in the British Forty-Third Regiment of Foot, was acting as Military Secretary to Sir William Howe.

To William Peterson

Sir   Camp [White Marsh, Pa.] Decr 1 1777

In Consequence of Orders sent herewith you will be admitted to return to New York, on your Parole, you will therefore pay to Mr Commissary Williams the Money you borrowed of me at Philadelphia if convenient—if not please to pay Mr Lewis Pintard in New York on my Acc^t., as he can appropriate it to the use of our Prisoners there.

I am sorry that I have so many Complaints of Cap Longstreet having so dishonourably broke his Parole by leaving the officer sent with you, at Burlington and absconding into the County of Monmouth—Nothing but an aversion to Severity, could have prevented a proper retaliation on M^r. Longstreet, as soon at this matter was reported to me—I think it was using you all well—

Peterson was a prisoner of the Americans in Connecticut.

To Richard Prescott

Sir   Camp near German Town [White Marsh, Pa.] Decr 1 1777
    I have the pleasure to inform you that by an Agreement lately entered into between their Exc^{ys}. Genl. Washington & Genl. How, the latter is to return on Parole as many Officers of equal rank as we shall admit to go into New York &c on their Parole—
    As there is no Exception in this Agreement, I conclude you may be permitted to receive the Benefit of it, wherefore I take the earliest Opportunity of acquainting you with it, that you may enjoy your Liberty before the severity of the Season comes on—
    I have wrote to Mr Commissary Williams to provide a Sloop for expediting your Voyage to New York with the other Officers under his Care—I could have earnestly wished that it had been consistant with Genl. Howe's Ideas, to have extended this Indulgence to you long before this— As we expect Genl. Lee will be returned in Consequence of your Arrival, any Endeavours you may use for expediting his Enlargement will be very agreeable—

Prescott was a British Major General who had been captured by Lieutenant Colonel William Barton, in a daring raid on the night July 9, 1777.

To Ezekiel Williams

Sir,   Camp [White Marsh, Pa.] Decr 1st. 1777
    In Consequence of a mutual Agreem^t. between Genl Washington & Genl. Howe, I am to desire you will immediately forward all the Officers who are Prisoners of War under your Care, to the City of New York, by Water—It will be necessary to send some spirited genteel Officer, of Militia (or in the Continental Service, if any) with them, who must take a rec^t. from the Commissary of Prisoners, or Commanding Officer there, for them—Each Officer must previously discharge their Arrears due for Board & other Expences and also sign a Parole, copy whereof is enclosed, otherwise they are to remain behind—If Genl Prescott chooses to travel by Land, I have no Objection to any route you will with the advice of the Governor may appoint him—You will take the usual mode of appointing a Flag of Truce for the Sloop that takes the Prisoners to New York— Among the Officers sent you from hence was a Capt. Longstreet, who to his great dishonor, broke his parole on his Journey and left the Officer who

had the Care of him, and went upwards of 60 Miles in the Country among his friends and did not join them again till they arrived at Princeton—As every Thing of this kind ought to be punished, I think you had best confine the Capt. in close Goal, untill the Sloop is ready to sail, unless by his late Behaviour he has wiped away the Stain—Be pleased to let me know whether the Enemy had yet any Commissary with you, who finds Provisions for their Prisoners—And for the future you will please to reduce their Allowance to 12 oz of Beef and as much Bread p^r Man p^r Day our Prisoners being allowed no more—As I do not know where Mr Messereau is, I must beg you will forward the enclosed Letter as fast as possible—If you have any addition to your Prisoners since the last return, please to send a return forward without the least delay, as I am in great want of it—I must also desire that you will do your Endeavour to confine all the privates, Prisoners under your Care, and do not suffer any of them to work out of the Goal Yards—The cruel, savage, Treatment our Prisoners meet with, calls aloud for this just act of severity—I wish the Acc^t. of all past Expences in fav^r. of Prisoners of War, disbursed by your State, could be forwarded on with dispatch—Be so good as to call on the Governor and let me know from him what has been done with regard to Mr Wallace, Philips & others, of which I have not heard a word—If Genl Prescott could be sent off a Week before the rest, it would not be amiss

To Robert Lettis Hooper Jr.

Sir   Camp [White Marsh, Pa.] Decr. 4th 1777

     I am very anxious to have the return of the Prisners under your Care on the 1st. of Novr last, as the Genl calls for the return of the whole.

     I should also be glad to know whether they are fed by a Commissary under Mr Franks or not—I am distressed by the Complaints of Travellers & the Friends of our Prisoners in Philadelphia, concerning the Prisoners in Easton being allowed to go at large—One retaken yesterday & examined at Head Quarters gave information that he was one of three who were cutting wood in your Service, and gott off, and he only was retaken on our Lines—Our Prisoners are close locked up & treated most cruelly—Be pleased immediately to confine all with you and if your Goals &c are not sufficient to hold them with safety, send the Surplus on to Reading—

     I have been detained here by a negotiation between the two Generals which has come to nothing at last—I expect to go for York in a couple of days—You will please for the future, not to suffer the Prisoners to receive more than 12 oz of Beef and as much Bread p^r Man p^r day that being the Quantity the Enemy pretend our Prisoners receive—

To Elisha Lawrence

Sir   Camp [White Marsh, Pa.] Decr. 4th 1777

As an Exchange of Prisoners on Parole is now negotiating between our two Generals, I think proper to remind you of an old Debt which remains due to me from you, being the amount of the monies you rec^d. from M^r. Willet in the Action at the Suit of Jos. Leonard—Altho' I do not mention the paym^t. of this money as a Term for your releasem^t., yet I doubt not, but you will have honor enough to leave me your Engagm^t. to pay the Ballance due, to M^r. Lewis Pintard who can appropriate it to the use of our Prisoners in New York—I ask this with more propriety, as you have rec^d. the money so long ago—

I did not choose to mention this Matter to you while there was no Prospect of an Exchange, but there can be no impropriety in it now—

Yours &

Lawrence was a Colonel in the New Jersey Militia.

To Joshua Mersereau

Sir   Reading [Pa.] Decr. 14 1777

I rec^d. your favour of the 15th. of Novr. not till within these two or three Days—As the Enemy were in sight on the rec^t. of the Letters, I ordered the Waggons to Easton where the loading will be stored—I am here on my way to Congress—have ordered Waggons into the Service, untill I return, when shall send them back to you—In Consequence of a Mutual Agreement between Gen^{ls} Washington & Howe, I am to desire you will immediately forward all the Officers who are Prisoners of War under your Care in Massachusets Bay & New Hampshire, into Rhode Island, by such Route as you think most convenient—It will be necessary to send some spirited genteel Officer with them who must take a rec^t. from the Commanding Officer there for them specifying their rank &c Each officer must previously discharge all Arrears for Board & other Expences and also sign a Parole, a Copy whereof in enclosed, otherwise they are to remain behind—They also bear their own Expences to R Island. You will make known these orders to the General, and be very exact in taking returns of all that are sent off & transmit them to me as quick as possible with the rec^ts for the Of[ficers] as our Prisoners will be confined till I receive them—I have repeatedly wrote for a return of all Prisoners in the Massachusets Bay, The Service suffers greatly for want of it—I must beg you will not loose a Moments Time in forwarding me a Compleat return, and if possible also of those in New Hampshire & Rhode Island Goverm^t—If you cant send the Names in these two last States, let me have an Estimate of their Numbers—let this be the first Business you do—You will remember that by a late resolve of Congress, all Sailors & Sea Captains wether taken privateers or others are all Prisoners of War & are to be taken Charge of accordingly—Let me know how the Prisoners are supplied with Provision, by whom & at what rate—

for the future you are not to allow them to receive more than 12 oz. of Beef & as much Bread p^r Man p^r Day, and whereever in your Power they are to be closely confined & not suffered to go without the Yards of the Goals—Great Disatisfaction is given, by the report of partial Exchanges being made the different Eastern States, particularly by a Vessel lately arrived at New York with 146 Prisoners—Pray let me know how this stands & suffer no Exchange of Prisoners of War without my Knowledge Extraordinaries excepted—Whenever you find the Prisoners with Provisions be carefull of taking proper rec^ts. for the rations delivered every week & keep regular Enteries of their coming & going out—As your Appointment is for the whole State, you can nominate the necessary under Officers in the different departments, but you must be very carefull not to nominate any unnecessarily or that can be done without—I wrote you of the 14th of Novr. which I hope you have rec^d. & forwarded the return—You will not forget that the above Orders for sending in the Officers, have no reference to those who surrendered w^h. G. Burgoyne

As for News I suppose you will hear strange Stories e'er this reaches you—On friday Morning about three oClock, the alarm Guns announced the Enemy's Approach—We were previously prepared for them on a ridge of Hills extending Eastwardly & westwardly at a place called White Marsh about 5 miles from German Town—Our Position was the best chosen possible, and our Troops sufficiently numerous & in high Spirits—About 8 °Clock they appeared in Sight on the opposite Hills—Their great Boasts of driving us beyond the blue Mountains, and every Preparation & Movement, such as General Howe & other Principal Officers coming out, all the Troops drawn out of the City, that could possibly be spared, & the great number of field Pieces, all bespoke their fixed determination to fight us—This led our Generals to keep their Posts on the Hills (where in Case of an Attack, in all human probability w^h the comon blessings of Heav^n a Compleat Victory must have attended us) at least till the Enemy shew any inclination to decline a Battle in w^h Case I believe they had determined to have begun the attack than suffer them to go into the City again without disturbance—Saturday Sunday & Monday was spent in slight Skirmishing & many Maneuvres of the Enemy from our Right to the left—By this Time they began to abate in their Ardour for fighting, and we begin to think of forcing them to Action—On Monday Evening they took Post directly in front of our Centre, kindled up a long line of fires & then silently & precipitately retreated to the City—Being deceived by the fires, we did not discover this Maneuvre till it was too late to come up with them with the Infantry, and could harass their rear very slightly with a few light Horse—Thus ended that high Threatinings with which the British Army had been filling the Ears of the Citizens of Philadelphia for several Weeks—Our Army is now gone into Chester County, this side of the Schuylkill not being able longer to supply with with forage &—I suppose the whole Loss of the Enemy in their late March was about 1000—Ours ab^t. 40—

To Robert Lettis Hooper Jr.

Dr Sir   Reading [Pa.] 14 Decr. 1777
    I am at last here in my Way to Congress—Your two favours of Novr. 28 & 29 have just been handed to me, enclosing the Return Parole &c.—I am greatly surprized at the order of the Council of Safety, who must certainly have been unacquainted with Coll. Duyckink being a Prisoner of War, or they never could have issued so absurd an order—
    You are not to obey any Order but from the Congress, Board of War, Commanding Officer of the Army or myself—I do not mean by this, that if a request should come to you from the Civil Authority, setting forth that a Prisoner of War was an Offender ag^t the State & requiring the Delivery of him to the Civil Officer, that it should not be complied with—I would do it without hesitation, but the present Order differs widely—
    I rec^d a Petition from a Thos. Limpers of Maryland which if true in point of facts, entitles him to lenity. Lest we should injure and innocent

Man by keeping him at Easton, must beg you will forward him on with the first Party to M^r. Attlee at Lancaster & desire him to send him to the Commissary in Maryland, that he may be heard before the Governor, who will release him or remand him, as he thinks proper—If you have an Opportunity by any party returning to Jersey, must beg you will send Joshua Mesereau & John Charlton to the Commanding Officer at Eliza. Town, with a desire that he will examine into their former Character & State of their Case, and if he thinks it prudent, to discharge or remand them as he finds they deserve—

I find by yours of Decr. 7th. that you paid the Officers guarding the Prisoners from Monmouth their Expences—In future pay no Acc^{ts}. of this Nature, unless coming thro' a Country, where they cannot draw Provisions as it is the Officers duty to draw from the Commissary the necessary rations, and a contrary Practice will give us a great deal of additional Trouble, by swelling our Acc^{ts}.

I am obliged to defer sending any Cash till I return, when I shall forward you a proportion of what I get—

Am &

To Richard Graham

Sir,   York Town [Pa.] Decm^r 22 1777

Your favour of the 26 Ultmo was delivered to me just as I was leaving camp and your Messenger not calling on me again was the reason I did not answer it by him—

I was much surpris'd at not hearing from Mr Lane before, it being the first Notice I had of his Resignation

I have consulted the Board of War on the Contents of your letter, and they think there must be some mistake in Mr Holmes informing you that they alledge that all the Prisoners East of the Bridge were under your Care, as this is the first Instance of their ever hearing of it—It being altogether incompatible with your Agency for Mr Franks would at all Events render your holding the office of deputy Commissary impossible— If you have had the Management of the Prisoners since Feby. it has been without the Knololedge and ag^t the Inclination of the Board of War or any of the Persons acting under them but on no other Acc^t. than your acting as agent for the British Commissary—I will write to Mr Holmes to take the Charge of all the Prisoners in Virginia as the Board does not choose to

have more than One—
 I shall enclose of M^r. Holmes Copies of some late Resolutions made by Congress, which concerns your department
 The Army is gone into Winter Quarters along the Hills on the Schuylkill so as to cover both sides of the river. They Hutt instead of Tents—There has been an arrival to the Eastward of a valuable Cargo on Acc^t of Congress viz 48 brass 4 Pounders 19 brass 9 Inch Mortars—2500 Shell 2000 4 lb Shot—9 Tons of Powder—3000 Stand of Arms—1110 fusees for Dragoons 61051 lb Brimstone & a parcell of Intrenching Tools.
 Am Sir   Your very Hum^l Servt

Graham had apparently been acting as a Deputy Commissary General of Prisoners in Virginia, but did not have a proper appointment. See Boudinot to Joseph Holmes on December 23.

To William Buchanan

Sir,   York Town [Pa.] Decm^r 22 1777
 Being authorisd by the Board of War to call on you for an immediate Supply of Provisions for our unhappy Prisoners now with the Enemy in Philadelphia and being un willing to encrease your difficulties in supplying the Army, I must beg the favour of you when you arive at Baltimore to ingage some proper Person to purchase without delay 500 Barrell of good fresh flour and forward it with the utmost dispatch across to New Castle or the nearest Water Carriage with orders to have them immediately shipped for Philadelphia—No delay must be suffer'd in the Business as the Lives of our brave and worthy Citisans depend upon it—I inclose proper Passports for the Purpose—The Sloop that Carries it must take a White Flag and call on the first Ship of War she meets with and shew the Credentials—If the Enemy should come to New Castle while it is there application must be made to the Commanding officer and a Protection Solicited—I should be glad of a few lines from you by the first Opportunity to Head Quarters that I may know how you are likely to succeed—
 If there is no Sloop to be got at New Castle I will send one from Philadelphia on having notice of it. The flour must be sent in my name to Thos Frankling Merch^t in Philadelphia. If the whole cannot be sent at once let it be sent at different Times—

I am with due Respect Your very Humb Servt
P.S. If the whole cannot be sent at once let it go at diff^t. Times, & if the river should freeze so as to prevent the Navigation, be so good as to direct its coming by land from the Head of the Elk—

Buchanan was Commissary General of Purchases. It was his job to provide food for the Continental Army.

To Joseph Holmes

Sir,   York Town [Pa.] Decr 23^d 1777
    Your favour I duly rec^d. and in Answer thereto I should send you full Instructions, would my Time at present by any Means allow, but the calls of my office prevents it, must therefore defer it, till I arrive at Camp when you shall have them with your deputation of a proper Date—M^r. Graham wrote me, that he has had the Care of the Prisoners on this side of the Ridge since last Spring—This must be a Mistake, as it would have been incompatible with his acting as an agent to M^r. Franks, and the Board of War know nothing about it—I shall therefore consider you as the deputy Commissary Genl. of Prisoners for the State of Virginia and desire you will take the whole Charge, by appointing proper Persons to take care of them at the different Posts, to whom you must make a reasonable allowance—You will please to send me without delay a return of all the Officers with you their Corps & Time when & place where taken if you Can—

Holmes was Deputy Commissary General of Prisoners for Winchester, Virginia and vicinity.

To Thomas Johnson

Sir,   York Town [Pa.] Decr. 23^d. 1777
    Being an entire Stranger to the inhabitants of your State, and under the necessity of appointing a deputy Commissary Genl. of Prisoners for Maryland, I am obliged to trouble your Exc^y in asking the nomination of a proper Person for that office, who shall receive his Appointment immediately—As I find fort Frederick is to be fitted up for their reception, I should be glad if he was acquainted with that part of the Country, a Man

of Character, Integrity & Activity—His Pay & rations will be that of a Major in the Army of the united States—As soon as he is nominated & accepts it, I shod be glad if he would immediately make out & send me an Exact return of all the Prisoners of war in your State with their Corps Time when & Place where taken—I have the honor to be &

Johnson was Governor of Maryland.

To George Lindenberger

Sir,   York Town [Pa.] Decr. 23^d 1777

Your favour of the 13 Inst. has just been handed me by the Board of War, in Answer to which, I must inform you that your Conduct with regard to the Hessian Prisoners has been approved of and as I am about to call in all the Prisoners, beg you will direct them to be sent by the first Guard that shall be coming this way, to this Town—Mr Lemon should bear the Expence of their return, but if he refuses, you are nevertheless to forward them on, and the Board of War must settle that matter with him—Direct the Prisoners to Thos. Peters Esqr. Commissary of Prisoners in this Place—
    Am &

Lindenberger was at Baltimore, Maryland.

To Ezekiel Williams

Sir,   York Town [Pa.] Decr 23^d. 1777

I wrote you lately to send in all the Officers Prisoners with you to New York, I am now by order of Congress to require you, to keep back any Captains of Men of War that may be in your State, and also such officers as have been taken since your return to me in July last and who belong to the New Levies raised in this Country, or the Militia.

It is meant that no others should be sent in till farther orders, than Genl Prescott & such British Officers as you have under your Care—

I write by this Opportunity to Mr Mesereau, and if the Messenger does not go on to Massachusets Bay, I must beg you to send an Express with it, so as not to loose an hour—
    Am &

P.S. I think you had best keep back L^t. Lundy if he is with you—

To Robert Haughy

Sir,   Camp Valley Forge Decr 28 1777

M^r. Sprogel has communicated to me, a Memorandum of your having a Quantity of flour to dispose of, besides Wheat Corn &c I am in immediate want of 500 or 1000 Barrels of good flour for the use of our unhappy Prisoners in Philadelphia; will therefore take what quantity you have, if you will engage to send it to your nearest Navigation, and then employ Boats to carry it down to Philadelphia, & for all your extraordinary Trouble, you shall be fully paid—

I should choose you should set about it without the least delay, for fear the River should close; in case this should happen, then the flour must be carted by Land, either to our Army that may be nearest, or quite down to the City, as you shall be directed hereafter—I will supply you with proper Passports for the Boats & Waggons passing and repassing to the City in safety—

You will please therefore to let me know by ye Bearer, who is sent Express for this purpose w^t Quty you can furnish me with, w^t. distance you are from navigable water & whether you will undertake to forw^d. it or, w^h you may begin to do, without any further orders. You can call on any Magistrate or Quarter Master who will press such Waggons as may be necessary & you may Engage them the same pay as the Continental Waggons receive—I will also pay you the same Price for the flour as the Com. of Purchases gives, besides all other Expences. Let me know by the Bearer w^t. Quty of Corn, Oats &c you have to Spare &

I am &c

Haughy was a merchant below Newark in New Castle County, Delaware.

To Thomas Franklin

Sir,   Camp [Valley Forge] Decr. 29 1777

Some time since, I had a meeting with M^r. Ferguson Commissary of Prisoners for the british Army, when I nominated you as an Agent for distributing such Provisions & other necessaries as might be sent in to our

Prisoners with you—M^r. Ferguson was pleased with the nomination, and I am now acquaint you [*sic*] of it, having been absent ever since, or you should have heard from me sooner—I hope this little Business will not be disagreeable, and for which you shall be generously rewarded, and you will thereby have an Opportunity of exercising a Degree of humanity to the unfortunate, which otherwise might have been out of your Power—

I send herewith under the Care of M^r. Clymer dpty Com. of Pris: a parcel of Flour & a number of fat Cattle [margin note 32 Blls 12 Cattle]— You will be pleased either to distribute the flour in Rations to the Prisoners, or sell it and divide the money as you see fit, so as to answer the most immediate relief to these brave but unhappy Men—I mean to keep you well supplied with flour for this Purpose, so as to answer all their necessities, and beg that they may want for nothing, that may make them Comfortable, as far as the supplies sent may enable you to aid them—The Beef you will give out at proper Seasons as long as it lasts, to the Prisoners to answer as a Charge to their salt Provisions—I mean what is now sent for immediate use—I have ordered a larger Quantity to be sent forward to New Castle & Christeen, to go up the Delaware with directions to deliver it to you, which when rec^d., I hope will serve as a full Supply—If the Navigation should be closed I have ordered it down by Land—I should be glad to hear from you as fast as it arrives—You will be pleased to keep your Accounts, so as to ascertain what each Prisoner receives, that it may hereafter be duly settled—Whatever the Inhabitants who are in confinement (but not Prisoners of War) may receive, must be kept separately from the Prisoners of War—Let me have an Acc^t. of what the prisoners want, and what supplies you think necessary that you cannot provide for them—

To Joshua Loring

Sir   Camp Valley Forge 29th. Decr. 1777
     Your Letter inclosing the Paroles & Exchange was received on my Way to York Town, from whence I am just returned—
     I am sorry to find that you have not included Capt Goodwin & the rest of the Gent^n. you say are gone to Canada, as those Officers went into New York, and all belong to the british Army, I cannot see why they should not be Exchanged in any department, and as to the Hostages who have been admitted on their Parole, I hope you are satisfied on this Head

& will include them in the Exchange—I must insist on Capt. Vandyke being released, as he is entitled to it from the Time of his Capture, and his being kept in the Provost so long, contrary to the usage given to your Officers with us, is an additional reason for his present releasement—I must therefore desire T^t he may be sent out for Capt M^{ac}Pherson—I would enclose the Paroles of those you sent me, who are not entitled to their Exchange yet, but my Papers are at a distance in the rear of the Army, and I cannot get them Time enough for this Opportunity

I have ordered Major Genl Prescott, with the rest of the british Officers in Connecticut, to be sent into New York, in Consequence of an Agreement between our two Gen^{ls}. for an Exchange of Officers of equal rank on Parole—I hope no delay will be suffered in releasing Major Genl Lee on the Arrival of Genl Prescott and as the rest of the Officers in our Possession will soon go in, I shall send you by the next Opportunity, an Exchange for the whole, which I hope will be agreeable—As I have at Genl. Howe's request sent him returns of your Prisoners, I must beg you will transmit me returns of those with you belonging to us, as soon as you conveniently can, and I should in future be glad of constantly exchanging returns of all Prisoners, that they may be hereafter taken, without particular Application—

I am &

To James Nielson

Sir   Camp Valley Forge Decr. 29 1777

I am just returned from Congress, where I have been a considerable time, or should have answered your favour sooner.

As the State have now affixed Prices to flour, wheat &c I must beg you will please to get what flour you can, and any other Articles, I before mentioned—I expect to go to Jersey in about 10 Days, when I shall let you have what money you may want

If the River should freeze up, it must be carted to amboy, & if Teems cannot easily be got, I have Authority from Congress to have them pressed—As our brave unhappy fellow Countrymen are perishing for want of full Supplies, beg you will exert yourself on this Occasion—

Am &

Nielson was at New Brunswick, New Jersey.

To Lewis Pintard

My Dr Sir   Camp Valley Forge Decr 29 1777
  I arrived here the night before last from Congress, and am fav^d. this moment w^t y^r Letter of the 22^d. Ins^t and am very glad of the Services you have rendered our brave tho' unfortunate Prisoners with you—I am now authorized & enabled to furnish them with every Thing comfortable—I shall therefore in about a Week, go for Jersey, when I shall take every Measure in my Power to replace all your Expences and endeavour to enable you to fulfill the Engagements you have made in their Behalf. We have been much discouraged, on lately being informed, that you have been prevented getting the Current Price for the flour, by a Measure designed only to affect the flour sent in by us—This is rather unworthy a publick Magistrate and will in the end be of no Service to them—You will for the future treat all Sailors as you do the Prisoners of War, as well to Cloathing as other Particulars—Passports have been refused for sending flour from Maryland, therefore we must send it from the States of Jersey & York.
  when you are able I could wish all the Officers in the Provost, were as well supplied as you can afford—If I can conveniently, when I get to Jersey, will send you in a few good Beeves for this Purpose, as also for the sick—If you supply any of our Inhabitants (not Prisoners of War) who may be in Confinement, keep a separate Acc^t. of it, so that it may be settled by the diff^t. States—I hope you will not suffer by my delay here for a couple of Weeks, as the necessity of the Prisoners in Philadelphia requires it—I have ordered into New York Major Genl Prescott & sev^{ll}. Officers from Connecticut (in Consequence of an Agreem^t. between Genl. Washington and Genl. Howe) for whom we expect Genl Lee and the oldest Officers in Captivity, of equal rank, will be sent out—the whole are only on Parole—I have sent for the other Officers in our Custody, who will go into the diff^t. Posts, for those of our Prisoners of equal Rank—It is sometime since I heard from home but believe that are all well. M^r R never paid me the Ballance due to you, but as he is in Phila: you had best settle with him immediately—
    Am &c

Enclosed you have the following Sums for our officers
Col Robt Magaw 7 half Jos.—Cap David Lennox 6 half Jos—Coll. S Atlee 4 d^o. Lieu^t. Gab. Blakeney 4 D^o. & 3 Eng. Guineas—Major Tarlton

Woodson a little bag sealed—Cap. Thos. Campbell 3 1/4-1/2 Jos & 3 Guineas—Saml. M^{ac}Eheltor 1 half Jos. 1 Moidore 1 Doll. 4 Eng. Shill., 5 small pieces silver—Capt. Snyder 5 1/4 half Jos. 22/6 Silver—

To John Adam

Sir,   Camp Valley Forge Decr. 30 1777
    I am just ret^d. from York Town and have but a few Minutes to desire you will endeavour to get a few hundred Barrells of flour, if to be had at 35/ or under and send them to New York to M^r. Pintard for the use of our unfortunate Prisoners—Also a dozen good fat Cattle for the same purpose—If you find any difficulty in obtaining them, call on the Commissary of Purchases for them—I have an order from Congress to get what I want of them—I also send by this Opportunity a Letter to Govr. Clinton from Congress, to give you all the Aid in his Power—You must wait on him, & he will direct you to such measures as will I dare say be effectual—
    If you can get any Thing from the State for their Inhabitants who are confined, but not Prisoners of War, forward it on to M^r. Pintard and let me have a particular Acc^t. of it—
    I lately rec^d a letter from M^r. Ab. Banker, informing me of his appointm^t to the office of Comm. of Pris. for the State of N York, and that he has disposed of the Prisoners in different Places—He desired also my Confirmation of his Appointm^t.
    I have wrote him for Answer that you were already Appointed, & that I desired him to deliver up all the Prisoners to you, which you will take Charge of & make return to me without delay—Not a Word of News here—I am informed that Coll. Delancey's Parole was taken, for his remaining at Hartford & within Six Miles—never suffer any parole to be taken again but to remain at such Place as shall be so appointed him by the proper Officer & within one Mile of it, or such other Limits as may be assigned him
    The sooner Provision gets into New York the better, & if a Boat load of wood could be sent o[r e]ven two of them, if to be had at a reasonable rate, I should be glad—

To Joshua Messereau

Dr Sir,   Camp Valley Forge Decr 30 1777
   I wrote you lately from York Town, from whence I am just returned.
I have rec^d. orders to build a set of Barracks immediately on Connecticut
River, with the advice of Govr. Trumbull, copy of Order is enclosed—As I
have made a great Noise about the Expences of the Barracks to the
Eastward, in justice to my own Character I must see that these are done in
the cheapest manner—I design them to be built w^h. Logs; to have them
low & strong—I propose that you should, when at leisure go to
Connecticut & advise with Govr. Trumbull & Mr Williams upon the Plan
& Place where—But would it not be best before a Word of it is known
abroad, to go near the Place where it is to be built, & purchase a good
piece of Woodland, with the Spot included for the Building—This
Woodland may furnish the Logs & afterwards answer for fire wood—As I
have no orders to purchase the Woodland, you may do it in my Name and
if the publick does not approve it, I will keep it myself—Let the Govr
certify the Price to be reasonable—If the Woodland cannot be got near the
Spot, let it be done on the River, that the Logs may be floated down, and
let Land fit for firing be purchased nearer—I mention these Purchases on
the Supposition, that they may be made reasonable—And if you think it
worth while, you may purchase a little farm near it between us, if you
think it would be profitable—You will draw up the Plan as soon as
possible and send it to me, with an Estimate of the Expence—They are to
hold 1500 to 2000 Men, to be well piqueted in, with a large Ditch round it
& Block Houses in the Corners—However I leave it to your Judgement,
to propose any Improvement you may think of, that will not greatly raise
the Expence—Building with Logs will save a vast Expence of Iron &
Nails and a Covering with good Cedar Boards might do, instead of
Shingles—I would not Dovetail the Logs, but by raising Bents would let
in the Logs with Mortice & Ten[an]t, which with a good Stone foundation
& strong Sills would answer very well—
   I am astonished at not receiving any returns of the Prisoners in Mass.
Bay—The Service suffers greatly for want of it & many poor fellows are
in close confinement for no other reason, but the want of these
returns—An Exchange on Parole is now stopped till it arrives—I hope it is
on the Way as both the General & Board of War have been calling for it
so long—

I am distressed to find that not withstanding all I can do, Exchanges are still carrying on to the Eastward, in so unjustifiable a Manner; by which means the greatest Clamours are rising among those Officers & their friends, whose turn is lost by this Partiality—I must beg, that you will by no means suffer an Exchange to take Place, or any Officer to go into New York, under any Pretence (without some very extraordinary Circumstance) unless I am first acquainted with it, as the utmost Confusion will otherwise arrise—The Enemy positively refuses to let any of our People in to see the State of our Prisoners, or any of them to come out for Cloaths or any thing else, and we must treat they as they treat us—

Am &c

To Richard Peters

Sir,   Camp Valley Forge Decr. 30 1777

On my Arrival here, I immediately set myself to work, to obtain Provisions for our suffering Bretheren in the City—I am much afraid it will be without Effect, or at best but a Scanty one, however I will exert every Nerve to accomplish it if possible—I called on the Presid^t. & Councile of this State but the only Answer I rec^d. was that Genl Washington had full Powers for the Purpose—This Scarcity seems the Harder as such large Quantities lye spoiling on the Banks of the Susquehanna—Enclosed you have Copy of a letter from M^r. Pintard (rec^d. this day by Express) for the Information of the Board of War—I am disturbed beyond measure, to see the sufferings of our poor Soldiers here for want of Cloathing—I am told that upwards of 3000 are returned unfit for duty for want of Cloaths to go out with; and indeed I have seen some myself, in this severe Season, whose bare Skin thro' their Breeches, and other rags has made me Shiver—An Officer just left me, who tells me, that out of 70 Men, only 6 can do duty for want of this necessary of Life—The clamours are rising so high that I fear the Consequence—I cannot help mentioning these facts tho' out of my department—I wish every Shoe in the State could be collected—small delays are dangerous—

Am &

P.S. The last 5 weeks we have sent away 150 Prisoners of war & about 100 Deserters—

Jan^{ry}. 1 1778

I enclose copy of a Letter from M^r. Ferguson—what shall I do for Blanketts for our poor fellows in the City, if they will not suffer them to be purchased there—I am afraid they will perish with the Cold as has been the fate of poor young Bayard—

Since the writing the above, I have rec^d. from Genl Washington the enclosed Copies of Letters from Genl. Robt Howe, by which you will see what faith is to be kept with rebells—You will observe by M^r. Pintards Letter that there has been another Exchange from Connecticut, if this irregular Mode is not stopped, the greatest Confusion must ensue—Capt. Trowbridge was Exchanged six months ago for a Capt then sent in— another now is sent for him without my Knowledge—A Lieutenant is sent in for Mr Callander who was only a Cadet in our Service—The greatest Complaints are made by our Officers of this unfair dealing, by whose management it has been done I know not—It grieves me to report to you, that so great is the distress for Cloathing, that unless some remedy can be immediately fallen on, I doubt the possibility of keeping the Army together Six Weeks longer—a few days past 21 Deserters came in one Day—I have sent in 32 Barrels of flour and 12 Cattle, for our prisoners, which were all that could be spared—

To Ezekiel Williams

Sir,   Camp Valley Forge Decr. 30 1777

Your fav^r. of the 8 Ins^t. has just been handed to me on my return from York Town, and am glad to receive the return enclosed, as I much wanted it—I find so much to do on my arrival here, that I can only write in a hurry—will send you the resolutions of Congress as soon as I get a little Leisure, with Instructions &c I have been sensible of the difficulties arrising from the want of Barracks, and will therefore endeavour to remedy it as soon as possible—When Mr Messereau has time, will direct him to call on you & consult with the Govr. on the Subject—I am sorry that Mr Messereau consented to suffer Capt. Mooney or any other, to go into New York, as the Enemy will not return the Compliment—I beg that no Exchange may be allowed on any Principles whatever, without my knowing of it, unless some extraordinary Circumstance should arise, and then only for such of our Officers as have been longest in Captivity— Great Offence has been given by this ungenerous mode of Exchanging

Officers thro' favour, & leaving many behind who are entitled from the Time of their Capture; it having been so often practiced to the Eastward, has raised loud Complaints from the other Officers, on which Acc^t. the Genl. has positively forbid any Exchange but in the order of Capture—I wrote this to M^r. Messereau & told him of it personally w^h made me think he would have put a stop to it; but by a Letter just rec^d. from New York, find that 3 or 4 Officers from your State has just been Exch^d., so that I know not where to call for a Person to be Exch^d. as I often find it done long before—

You are not to allow any Prisoner of War to send in for any Paper Bills, but in Case of any Considerable Quantity coming out, you are to stop it, as the Enemy have Counterfeited our Money & publickly advertised it for Sale—I desire you will not suffer the Officers to send or receive Letters at any rate from New York or elsewhere, unless they pass thro' your Hands let them know that if they are discovered either writing or receiving Letters by private hands, it will be considered as a Breach of their Parole & they will be closely confined.—Be so good as to enquire how M^r. Barton rec^d so large a Sum of money, as he had none when he went to Connecticut, and if you find out any private Correspondence he has had, or any large Sums remitted him, confine him at once, and take possession of his Papers & Money to be delivered him when he is returned to New York—Consult the governor on this Head & take his advice—

Since writing the above, yours of the 22^d. Ins^t. has been put into my Hands, and am very sorry for the Exchange of Capt. Mooney—you must see the great Confusion that will arise if any Person, besides the Congress or Commander in Chief can order an exchange of Officers without my Approbation—I have already clothed all our Prisoners in New York, and have ordered in Provision for them, so that they may live Comfortably this winter—I have an Agent there Lewis Pintard Esqr; who is a Man of great humanity & does all in his Power for them, to whom you may send any Thing, that their friends chooses, such as flour, Cloathes &c which he will either sell & distribute the money, or deliver the Provisons as he is directed—I am greatly distressed for Coll. Webbs fate, but I am forbid suffering any Exchange but according to the order of Time in which Prisoners are captured—Coll Campbell I have engaged shall only be Exch^d. for Col Ethan Allen—Whatever Effects any Officers, who have broke their Parole or may hereafter break it & leaves behind, you will be pleased to seize & make report to me—No Officer ought to have more than one Mile, but I will report the matter to Congress, & get a Stop put to Generals taking Paroles at any rate—I have wrote to Mr Messereau to consult you about the Barracks & also w^h the Govr and to send me your Opinion, that they may be set about immediately—

 Am &c

To Henry Hugh Fergusson

Sir   Camp [Valley Forge] Decr. 31st. 1777

 Being just returned from York Town, I am favoured with your Lre of the 19th. Ins^t. and shall immediately set about sending in the necessary Supplies for our Prisoners—With this I for^d. a few Waggons loads of flour and a few fat Cattle for their immediate relief, till I can have a little Time to settle matters for a regular Supply—While absent I ordered a parcell of flour to New Castle & Christeen, to go up the Delaware as the most effectual mode & the least liable to objections, but in Case the navigation should be stopped, then to be forwarded by Land—I have given Directions that the Sloop shall call on the Commanding Officer of the first Ship of War, that they meet with, and shew him their Orders and take his Directions—The whole as it gets in, is to be delivered to M^r. Thos. Franklin, agreeable to what pass'd between us, when on the Lines—

 Genl. Howes Surprize that no returns of y^r. Prisoners had been made might have been prevented, by adverting to what I told you, and what was also mentioned in the rough Estimate given to you, viz That previous to the request made for those returns, all my Books, Papers &c were sent off to Congress, whither I was bound when ordered to Philadelphia—I also mentioned my Knowledge of Genl. Howe's request, when I informed you that the rough Estimate was made for Genl. Washington on receiving his orders for making out the return for Genl Howe—

 You have herewith the returns of your Prisoners amounting to 2400; those in Massachusetts Bay, Rhode Island, New York & Maryland, I am not able to send with this—The Prisoners having been lately ordered there, and altho' I have directed the returns to be sent to me, they are unaccountably delayed; but as I receive them, they shall be sent—from the best Judgement I can form, the numbers in the whole, will be very near the Estimate I sent you, notwithstanding you suppose, that these are but little more than half the number in Captivity—Those in New York State are principally in the Hospital at Albany, and a few foreigners, amounting to about 400 as I am informed—

It gives me some uneasiness, that these returns now sent are so informal, I did not discover it, till they were finished and it was too late to have them better done—I have lately seen a number of your Prisoners, at the different Places of their Confinement, and they all want of every Kind of Cloathing many of them almost naked, but in general they are most in want of Blanketts (of which they have none) Shirts & Shoes—The Hessians in particular complain exceedingly, thinking themselves forgotten by those who have the direction of their Cloathing & Pay. Many of the Prisoners must certainly perish, if their clothing is not sent out speedily—

Some time the beginning of November, I mentioned the case of the Hessians taken at red bank in a very particular manner, as their Cloaths were scarcely fit for Summer and I sent the report of the Surgeon of the Hospital, relative to them, but have never yet rec^d. even an acknowledgm^t. of the rec^t of the Letter, which indeed has been universally the Case, whenever I have given information of the wants of your Prisoners, unless in a single Instance—

I hope you are by this Time in possession of the Papers relative to our Prisoners, so that you can transmit me, the returns of them by M^r. Clymer dpty Commissary of Prisoners, who goes to your Lines with an expectation of being admitted to examine into the State of our Prisoners & their Wants, agreeable to Genl. Howes Letters; I hope to be able on his return to afford them proper relief—

Genl. Prescott and other british officers from Connecticut are gone into New York on the Agreement lately made between our two Gen^{ls}. and hope Mr Loring has got proper Orders for the release of Genl Lee and other Officers of equal rank on Parole (I mean those who have been longest in Captivity) in return—When the Officers from Virginia arrive, will send the few in this State with them to Philadelphia—

I enclose an Exchange, proposed on the above mentioned agreem^t. and hope it will be agreeable—

I am &

Fergusson, from Pennsylvania, had been appointed Deputy Commissary of Prisoners with Sir William Howe's army in November 1777.

To Joseph Holmes

Sir,   Camp [Valley Forge] Jan^{ry} 2^d. 1778
By an Agreement lately entered into between Genl. Washington &

Genl. Howe, the Officers in Confinement on both sides are to be exchanged on Parole—I therefore desire you will immediately forward on all the Officers Prisoners of War under your Care, to Lancaster in this State, to the Care & direction of W^m. Atlee Esqr. Commissary of Prisoners in that Town—You'll be please [*sic*] to take their Paroles, for their safe going in such route as you shall direct to that Place, and their abiding as true Prisoners of War till Exchanged—Then send them off under the Care of some spirited & genteel Person, who must see that they keep the proper road & do not wander unnecessarily through the Country.—They must first discharge all arrears & Expences due for Boarding, receipts for money, & other little matters otherwise they are to remain behind—I do not mean that they should be hurried off to travell in the midst of Winter ag^t their wills, but let them sett of when they please, provided they do it together. They are not to be allowed Horses or waggons but at their own private Expence—

The Prisoners are to be reduced to the allowance of 12 oz Beef or 8 oz Salt Pork & 12 oz Bread p^r Man p^r day & you are not to allow them to receive more. Nor is the allowance of two dollars p^r week to be allowed hereafter to any Officer whatever

Am &c

To Robert Haughy

Sir   Camp Valley Forge Jany 3 1778
I have but a few Moments to answer yours of the 28th Ultmo, it being necessary to send off the Bearer immediately on Acc^t of other Business— The flour I want must be fresh & good—You will be pleasd therefore to get 500 Barrells ready as fast as you can & send it down to port Penn—As soon as the Navigation is open, send it down in small Craft 2 or 300 Barrells at a Time—Enclosed you have two pass ports for the Purpose, you will be carefull to fill up the Dates & put in the Boatman's Name—He must carry a White Flag at his Bowsprits End & call on the first Man of War he meets with—If the flour gets down (I mean the first parcell) in Ten Days or two weeks, it may answer—After the 500 Barrells are got to the Landing, you shall hear farther from me about the other 500 before they are sent off—As to the Teams you Employ let them find their own Forage, and I will pay them the same that the Quarter Master Genl. does for Teams finding themselves, and if they are good Teams & are very active, perhaps a little more to drink my Health—I desire that you would

keep all your Corn & Oats, let the Quantity be what it may, and I will have it sent for—If you could send up to Philadelphia about Twenty or thirty Barrells of Beef & Pork, I should be glad, but it must be good & well cured—If you want money, you must let me know it and I will supply you—I shall go next week into the Jerseys, but on my return, will send you what you want—

In the mean Time direct your Letters to me or my Deputy, to be left at the Adjutant Generals Office in Camp, and if necessary they will be sent to me by Express—whatever you send is to be delivered by M[r]. Tho[s]. Franklin Merch[t]. in Philadelphia. I depend upon you to get Craft to take up the Flour from Port Penn—

Am &c

To Jesse Hollingsworth

Sir   Camp Valley Forge Janu[ry]: 4th 1777 [1778]

The distress of our unhappy Prisoners, has given me so much uneasiness, that the recept of your Letter was particularly pleasing to me on finding that you was so far advanced as Wilmington—Enclosed you have two pass ports for Going into Philadelphia one of which with those for going by water you'll leave behind at Wilmington till you return you will not forget to fill up the date of the second now sent when you use it—

I must beg that you will keep Going either by land or water till you Get in 500 Barrels, and then stop till you hear father [sic] from me. I should be glad you could also send in (especially if you should Go by water) Twenty or Thirty barrels of Beef and Pork if to be had at any reasonable rate—as to money you can either get it of M[r] Buchannan or any purchasing Commissary or of my self, as it shall be most Handy—If I can Get a Safe Opportunity will send you here with 500 Dollars to bear the present extra Expence—I expect soon to Go to Jersey, but when I return will let you have what further Sum you want—you will please to engage your Brother to take charge of this Business, if you think he will answer—Direct your Letters to me or my Deputy to be left at the Adjutant Generals Office in Camp

you will deliver the Flower to M[r]: Tho[s] Frank Merchant Philad[a]. and take recept for the Same

I am Sir

Hollingsworth was a merchant from Elkton, Maryland, then at Wilmington, Delaware, on his way to Philadephia.

To Robert Lettis Hooper Jr.

D^r. Sir   Camp [Valley Forge] January 6th: 1778
      your several favours, one without date the Others of the 22^d & 24th:
Ultmo and 4th Janu^y: all Came to hand this day the last enclosing the Letter
from M^{rs}. Leonard—as to Thomas Simpson I am afraid he is greatly
deceived you with the aid of the Person who was sent to take care of him.
He Informd M^r: Attlee that he had not Seen him since he left East Town
Simpson has not Appeared since and I suppose has Gone off—
      The Congress have passed a Resolve that All Provision found for the
British prisoners shall be paid for in hard Money but as the resolve is very
Insufficiently drawn up, I shall write to Get it Altered before I send it to
you—I have by no means been Inattentive to Capt: Byles and have sent in
for his Exchange which I hope will be Affected—I am Glad you have
locked up the British Prisoners they will now be able to Convince the
British Army that even double the quantity of Provisions allowed to our
Poor Fellows Is not Satisfactory to their Stomachs my Humanity was long
put to the Trial before I could be brought even to the Orders you have
rec^d: I have tried every other mode but in vain we must now be resolute
and Firm and if this will not do shall be oblig^d: to reduce it still more I beg
the reason of it may be propagated Among them I pity the Subjects of this
severity and wish it was Consistant with Humanity to our brave Fellows to
Treat the English prisnors as well as I could wish but this will not be done
till an Alteration in their favour & am now oblig^d. to send in Provisions
both to New York & Philadelphia in Order to Keep our Prisoners from
Starving as many of them have done but I beseech you not to Suffer the
least Impertanance Amongst them the Letter Inclosd to me, is in so
threatning a strain that I think every Rascal of them should be put in Irons
I would have you keep a strong Guard round the Goal, and not Suffer any
person to Converse with them—If you can Possibly Keep these fellows a
week or two longer with Safety I should be Glad, as I hope by that Time
to have such a place ready for them that there will be but little difficulty in
Secureing them—
      I know not what to Say relative to the Hessians as I must Confine
them in a few days there being a determined Resolution not to Suffer one
of them to Go at large and it will Give Great Troble to be calling them in,
in a few days you may let the Prisnors write in to Philadelphia as many
complaints as they please—I know of no Complaints against you for want
of fidellity to the states they have arose from the friends of our unhappy

Brethren in Captivity whose feelings are very tender on this Occation against you me and Even the General for the lenety Shewn the Prisnors and as an Instance, the Liberty allowed them at East Town, was quoted more than once—

I cannot account for the difference between the two last lists sent me there being forty odd Difference you will please to reconcile them so that I may not make a Confusion in my Gener^r. Return—I have rec^d. M^{rs}. Leonards letter I feel Exceeding for the unhappy woman and Shall Write to her Enclosed & will forward her letter to Major Leonard

I am much Obliged to you for your Care of the Sugars & the Waggons. I had quite a different Design with these Sugars, but as they are now at East Town and I am so circumstanced that on the whole I must beg that you will add to the Other Obligations, I am Already Under by immediately Disposing of all Sugars excepting a Couple Flower Barrels of the best if one of the Casks weighs but five or Six Hundred will be pleased to Keep for me till you hear from me again

I must Get about £40 p^r C^t: to make any Profit by it—they cost £25 lawful in hartford Except a small part of it However I doubt not but you will do everything in your power for me &

To William Atlee

D^r: Sir   Camp [Valley Forge] January 7th: 1778
    Your favours of the 28th & 31st: Ins^t: came safe to Hand the 36 Barrels Flower Gave me very great Pleasure, as it added much to the relief of our unfortunate Bretheren I hope eer this day they Have near 200 Barrels in the City and more going in daly with a supply of very good fresh Beef I have been much more favoured in my Purchases of Flower then I expected from the reports I heard when at Lancaster I shall have 1000 Barrels in the City within a fort night as to Simpers if he has Gone off he must be a Deceitful Rascall, but I believe is no Great Loss—

    I enclose you a list of deputy Commissaries of Prisoners in the different States at least all that are now appointed

    When you forward Prisoners to the west ward which will now be the State of Maryland, instead of Virginia Direct them to Thomas Peters at York Town—I have not rec^d: your Enclosing the letters and Cash for Prisoners tho' I think it high Time—I sent the little girl into the City and

Expect the return of the waggon any moment Who will be the bearer of this—No news here but the taking of Several vessels on the Delaware after they ware drove aground by Ice one of them near Wilmington turns out a very rich prise she had on Board 1000 Stand of armes and very large quantity of Officers Baggage consisting of Several hundred Trunks & several Pipes of wine, Beer rum &c &c—I am sorry that I cannot Informd you the news that enlivened you relative to Genl Sullivans Success—you must not believe any report of feats done by Our Army till they can get Clothes to venture out of their Hutts it would make your heart ake to see our distress for the Necessary Articles of every kind of Clothing I must beg you to make my most respectable Compliments acceptable to M^{rs}. Attlee and the young Ladies and be Assured that I am with Great respect

To Thomas Franklin

Sir   Camp [Valley Forge] Jan^{ry} 8th. 1778
          Herewith will be delivered to you twelve fat Cattle, for the use of our Prisoners—The reason of my sending these in now, is my being obliged to go for Jersey, where I shall be absent some time & perhaps, more may not be sent in till my return—Let me know by the Bearer if you have rec^d. more flour by water—
          This sent by [Go]v^r. Chaloner—

To Henry Hugh Fergusson

Sir,   Camp [Valley Forge] Jan^{ry}. 8th. 1778
          Enclosed you have a return of the Hessians that were in the Hospital at Princeton, but are now sent to Easton, which I have rec^d since my last—The Bearer goes with a small Drove of fat Cattle, for our Prisoners, by whom should be glad of an Answer to my last relative to the Exchange then enclosed,—
P. S. I send for Louis Drew 18 Dollars & 1/2 Guinea—3 Dble Loons for Coll. Tolliver [probably Taliaferro] 1 D^o. 1 1/2 Jos. & 2 Guineas for Major O Towles sent afterwards 10 Dollars for L^t. Rufus Lincoln

To William Edmestone

Sir,   Camp [Valley Forge] Jan^ry. 8th. 1778
    In examining my Papers since you left me, I find an Account ag^t. you
of £ 48:15: for so much received by you of Coll Haller on the allowance of
two Dollars p^r week—As my Orders are not to suffer any Officer to be
Exchanged, untill their Arrearages are paid, the payment of this Debt falls
on me—I must therefore beg the favour of you to pay this money to M^r.
Thomas Franklin of Philadelphia or Lewis Pintard of New York, either of
whom will apply it to the use of our Prisoners there, and whose rec^t. shall
be your discharge—
    Am sir &

Edmestone was Major of the British Forty-Eighth Regiment of Foot was then in
Philadelphia. He had been a prisoner in Reading based on the reference to Henry Haller.

To William Govat

Sir   Camp [Valley Forge] Jan^ry 9th. 1778
    I have lately rec^d from the State of Massachusets Bay, the Accounts
of money expended for Prisoners of War by that State—On looking into
them I find the Charges for the maintenance of Prisoners on a March as
well as Allowances made the Officers & Guards escorting them, so far
beyond any thing I have ever been used to, that I have thought proper to
send them herewith, that the Treasury Board may examine & take such
Measures relative to them, as they may think proper.
    I have been very successfull in my purchases of flour since I have
been in Camp, for the use of our Prisoners in the City—I expect there are
already arrived there, about 450 Barrells of flour & 24 fat Cattle and that
1000 Barrells of flour will get there in a fortnight, so that I hope the
Prisoners will not suffer in future—
    I am &

Govat was Secretary to the Treasury Board of the Continental Congress.

To Robert Haughy

Sir   Camp [Valley Forge] Jan^ry 9 1778
    In Answer to yours of the 6th. Instant I enclose you four Passports,
for the Purpose of sending in the rest of the flour to Philadelphia—I also

send by the Bearer One Thousand Dollars, and when I return from Jersey will supply you with as much as you want—When you have got in the five hundred Barrells, you'll please to delay the rest, till towards the Middle of February, unless you hear sooner from me: or in Case you find any sudden Alteration in the Situation of our Troops at Wilmington, then push it in as fast as possible, that we may not henceforth be deprived of this mode of Conveyance—As fast as you send in any Quantity, let me know it by any Convenient Opportunity—I wish by the next Sloop you would send in about a Ton of Indian Meal ready Boulted, provided you can dry it, so as to prevent its spoiling Also a few Carcases of good Beef & Dozen Hogs—

I should also be very glad of your sending in about 20 Cords of good fire wood, or even thirty Cords, if it can be got at a tolerable Price—If you should want Passports at any Time, please to apply to Gen[l]. Smallwood or the Commanding Officer of the Troops at Wilmington, and he will give you them, of the same Tenor with the Enclosed, a Copy of which you had best keep by you—

Am &c

The Passports differ in the[   ]

P.S. Since writing the above, Gen[l] Howe had forbid any more Provisions in by water You will therefore Stop your Hand for the present till you hear from me—In the mean time forward what you can by Land whenever the Roads are good—I have wrote in remonstrating ag[t] this refusal & hope to get Liberty at least to send up the wood by water—

To Franciscus Sheffer

Sir,   Camp [Valley Forge] Jan[ry] 10 1778

Your Letter to his Exc[y]. Gen[l]. Washington has just been handed to me, as belonging to my department—You should be immediately suffered to go into Philadelphia for the Purpose you mention was it not agreed to have a general Exchange on Parole of all the officers in our Possession—You will therefore, by the Time this reaches you receive directions for coming with the rest of the Officers, to Lancaster in this State, where I shall either meet you or leave Directions for you.

I have repeatedly wrote to the English Commissary, a State of your wants & urged the necessity of sending down some Assistance to you, but have never rec[d]. any Answer—

Am &c

Sheffer, Lieutenant Colonel of the Hessen-Cassel Fusilier Regiment von Lossberg, had
been captured at Trenton, New Jersey. At this time he was being held in Virginia.

To Henry Hugh Fergusson

Sir   Camp [Valley Forge] Jan^{ry}. 10 1778
    In order that the Supplies designed for our prisoners might be more
compleat & to prevent the keeping up a continual Communication by
Land thro' the Lines, I directed a Quantity of Flour &c to be sent up the
Delaware not doubting but that it would be the most agreeable mode of
Conveying it I could fall upon, having previously informed you of my
Intentions—Your Silence on this Head, led me to believe that Genl. Howe
acquiesced in the propriety of it, I therefore have ordered down to the
Landing 7 or 800 Barrells of Flour, a ton of Indian Meal; 20 or 30 Cords
of Wood & a few Carcases of Beef & Pork, with orders to send them up
the Delaware, and do suppose some of the Articles are now on the way to
your City in different Sloops—It was not till this Evening on the rec^t. of
Genl. Howes Letter to his Exc^y Genl Washington, that I suspected it was
not approved of, I shall therefore put a stop to it as soon as the distance,
will permit, unless General Howe will permit those articles above
mentioned to be taken up the river, as they are already ordered to the
Landing, and perhaps the greatest part of them will be on their way before
I can possibly put a stop to it—I must beg the favour of a speedy Answer
that I may take my Measures accordingly—
It gives me pain Sir, that I am obliged to inform you, that it is expected
that after the first day of February next, you will supply all your prisoners
with us west of New Jersey with every kind of Provisions sent out from
your Lines, and that I have it positively in Charge, not to suffer your
Agents to purchase any Provisions in the Country after that day—The
proper Passports for your Conveying any Quantity you think proper to the
different Places of your Prisoners Confinement shall be ready whenever
you require them, and your Agents shall be allowed to distribute
Provisions & other necessaries as you may please to direct them—I shall
also take Care that our Prisoners with you, are fully supplied with
Provisions from hence, after that Day—As to fire wood, I will either send
a sufficiency to them, or supply your Prisoners in their different
Cantonments with as much for every Ten Men, as you shall assure me you
allow to every ten of ours—The Officers in like manner—This Measure

has become absolutely necessary, as it is rather unequal to suffer your Agents to purchase every kind of Provision at their Pleasure among us, while our Agent is refused the Priviledge of purchasing necessary Cloathing with you—If any Inconvenience should arise to the unfortunate Prisoners on this Acc[t]. it cannot be chargeable on us—

To Richard Peters

Sir   Camp [Valley Forge] January 11th: 1778
    Just now Setting off for Jersey I have only time to acquaint the board of War, that I ordered a thousand Barrels of flower to a landing on Deleware together with 30 Cords of wood and a quantity of Indian meal in Order to go up the River to Philadelphia have previously informed the Commissary of British Prisners with my Intentions
    In the mean time I sent in by land from below Wilmington and other Places, 168 Barrels of flower & 24 fat Cattle from this place for present use on the arrival of one sloop with 150 Barrels of flower at Philadelphia Gen[l]. Howe has wrote out forbidding any more provision to be sent in by water so that I shall be obligd to Send it quite from Port Penn By land
    I am Also Sorry to inform you that my Agent at Philadelphia Purchased or Agreed for a parcel of Blanket for the prisners but was obligd to give them up again on the most preemptory Order from Gen[l]. Howe that he would not suffer it—several of our Unhappy Prisnors have Died Merly for the want of Blankets and other Clothing and I know not where to Get a single Blanket or Suit of Clothing for their relief I have wrote in Giving the Enemy notice that they will not be Suffered to Purchase any kind of Provision with us After the 1st of February at least to the west werd of Jersey the reason of this Exception is the Liberty we have of Purchasing Cloaths at New york

To Jesse or Henry Hollingsworth

Sir   Camp [Valley Forge] Jan[ry] 11 1778
    Just setting off for Jersey, I can only inform you that Gen[l]. Howe has forbid any more Provisions going into Philadelphia by Water, therefore must desire you will forward the flour to the amount of 500 Barrells by Land to Philadelphia whenever you think the roads will answer—They are

not in want of at present, therefore you need not hurry yourself—I wish you to acquaint me from Time to Time, what Quantity you send in—You may add either Pork or Beef—Salt or fresh as you can meet with it. When the 500 Barrells get in, you shall hear from me concerning a farther Supply—If you want Passports apply to Gen[l]. Smallwood—

Am &

Henry Hollingsworth was a Deputy Quartermaster General at the Head of Elk, now Elkton, Maryland.

To Joshua Mersereau

Baskinridge [N.J.] Jan[ry] 16th 1778

I have at last sent off two waggons with one Ton of Bar Iron purchased of M[r]. James Hockley of Glascow Forge for £150 proc: I should have sent more but the Carters thought they could not get along with it—I sent this in preferrence to flower as it is on our joint account, having laid your letter before the Board of war and they would not give me any Orders to send it on the publick account which I certainly should have preferred I was informed by the Carters that being out of grain and supposing they were in my Service as a publick Officer they drew at different Quarter masters on the way about 30 bushells of Grain this now cannot be helped, but by paying the Commissary Gen[ll] of Forage for it, which shall do and charge it to our joint Acount—The waggons were employed in the Service while they remained here—I gave the Carters 60 Dollars to bear their Expences and have their receipt Accordingly, which shall also charge as above—I am exceedingly distressed for want of the return of prisoners from your States: you had better have paid £100 for them than to have had them kept back so long: The General is much displeased with the delay, as he is brought in to a dispute with General Howe for want of them. You also are much blamed for the neglect of sending them long ago. I beseech you to let me have them without delay, as the Service suffers greatly for want of them: if you can do no better, petition the President and Councill and let them know the misconduct of their Officers.—The Exchange suffered to the Eastward, raises such Clamours here, that a stop must be put to them at all Events, and no one must be allowed of without my Knowledge. Great Impropriety having been committed by this means, you must not allow officers any thing on the publick Account unless a single ration to those who are closely confined; the Congress having discontinued the allowance of two Dollars pr week. If they have Horses or Carriages it must be at their own Expence—I hope you have received my Letter from Reading & anot[her] from York Town I expect to remain here about three weeks if you could write me & order it left here perhaps it may meet me—

To Ezekiel Williams

Sir   Baskinridge [N.J.] Jan^{ry} 16 1778
     Your favour the the 4th Ins^t was just brought to me from Camp, being engaged here on a little Business—I am much surprized at your being yet without my Letter of the 1st. Dec^r, Copy of which is enclosed, and which was sent, I think by Post—I hope you have rec^d. it eer this, especially as I have heard that Genl. Prescott is arrived at New York—I do not wonder that you did not fully Comprehend my last Letter, without reading the one above referred to My design was that you should send in to New York, all the british Officers, you had under your Care, they first signing the Parole & paying up all arrears &c This I hope is already done, if not, the sooner it is done the better—I have sent to Genl. Howe a proposal for Exchanging all the Officers in our Hands on Parole, as he will not by any means agree to an absolute Exchange—I expected an Answer long ago, but am yet expecting of it, and if agreed to, shall then send in the new Levies, with every other Officer, that remains behind—As to Coll Bartons request, he is by no means entitled to any Thing beyond the common Treatment of a Prisoner of War, and must not be allowed any further Indulgence—If Genl Howe admits of his Exchange, he will then be immediately sent in—I have wrote to you lately, and beg now to repeat it, not to admit any Exchange, without letting me know of them, as the utmost Confusion must otherwise ensue, as the Instance you mention will fully evince—Captain Keating being the second Capt. now given for Capt. Trowbridge—It is now upwards of 4 Months since a Capt. Francis was sent in as an Exchange for Capt. Trowbridge, and till lately I thought he was at home with his Family, but now by this Artifice, the Enemy have got two for one—Also I am informed that a Lieutenant has been sent in for a Mr Callander who was only a Cadet in our Service—This Conduct of partial Exchanges has never been used, but by the Eastern States, which has given every just cause of heavy Complaints in the Army, and must not

be allowed hereafter by any Means—I have recd the Accounts of disbursements &c but have not leisure yet to examine them.

You will be carefull not to advance any Money to Officers on the publick Account, as the Congress have discontinued all allowance to them of every kind, unless they are close confined & then only a common Ration—They are not to be allowed either Horse or Carriage, but at their own Expence, and if they do not satisfy their Landlords, of the Certainty of Payment for their Board, they are to be confined in Goal—This is severe, but precisely on the Plan, the Enemy have marked out, in their treatment of our Prisoners, and my Orders from Congress are, to follow them exactly in every Step—As to L^t. Bloxham, you must not suffer him to be exchanged till he pays all he owes, and if he does not observe your directions with great Exactness keep him Continually locked up—As soon as I return to Camp, will write to York Town, for orders on your Loan Office in your favour—

If you have an Opportunity to write within [2] weeks, direct to be left at this Place, within about 7 Miles of Morris Town New Jersey—we have taken several Vessels lately in the Delaware, by the help of the Ice, one of which was very Valuable—Altho' it did not contain what was published in the News Papers, yet it was well worth the Capture—About 800 Stands of Arms—400 Tents—40 Marques—200 Trunks of Officers best Baggage—20 Pack Saddles—Rum—Wine & 62 Soldiers & 13 Sailors with two Officers—If you can forward M^r. Messereau's Letter sent herewith, you will much oblige me—

To John Covenhoven

Dr Sir   Baskinridge [N.J.] Jan^{ry} 17th. 1778

My Brother expecting to be the Bearer of this I have desired him to endeavour to see & Consult with you relative to the flour & wood to be sent to New York—I must again beg that you will exert yourself on this Occasion, and if you could add a few Quarters of very good beef (say 10 or 12) or 100 Bush^{ls}. of Indian Corn, please to do it—I enclose two Passports for the Sloop, and most heartily wish, she may go off with the first open Weather—

Covenhoven was in Monmouth County, New Jersey.

To Robert Dodd

Sir   Baskinridge [N.J.] Jan^ry. 17th. 1778

The Bearer M^r. Collins is sent Express to push on all the Flour you can possibly collect—I beg you will endeavour to send off immediately for Eliz. Town, what you have got—if you could get 100 or 200 Bush^ls. of Indian Corn it would be serviceable—I must also have a Dozen Head of large fat Cattle—These may be taken out of any Drove going to camp, or purchased in the Country—I have orders from Congress to call on any of the Purchasing Commissaries for this Purpose and Coll Buchannan ordered me to call on you particularly—If you could send down a few Hogs just killed & a few firkins of good Butter it would also be acceptable, and any kind of Salt provisions—I must beg you will exert yourself without delay, as our unhappy Prisoners are starving at New York—As every Thing arrives at Eliz. Town it must be delivered to the Quarter Master there—

I shall want 1000 Barrells of Flour, but hope to get some this way, but beg you will send all you can—If you have not a sufficient Quantity, direct the Bearer what Route to take, to call at as many Mills as possible, to secure what he can—This Supply may be made out of any flour engaged for the Army, and Sleds must be pressed for the immediate Conveyance to Eliz. Town, but it must be fresh if possible—I wrote you a few days past from Eliz. Town—

Dodd was an Assistant Commissary of Purchases based at Flemington, New Jersey.

To William Chamberlain

Sir   Baskinridge [N.J.] Jan^ry 19 1778

My Brother informs me that you promised him to let me have all the Flour you could possibly spare, for our unhappy Prisoners at New York—I have such melancholy Accounts of their Wants, that I am come from the Army on purpose to push in all the Provisions I can to them without Delay—

I must beg that you will immediately send to Eliz. Town all you have, or can purchase in your part of the Country—

You must apply to the proper Magistrate, to press all the Sleds that may be necessary on this Occasion, if they cannot be other wise obtained, altho' I should think no Man of humanity who knows the unhappy situation of our brave Country men in Bondage, but would willingly exert himself for their relief—

Please to direct the Bearer, where you think he can collect any more, if you have not enough—I imagine 1000 Barrells at present would be sufficient altho' I should be glad you would still be collecting as much more as you can—I hope Mr Dodd at Flemington can supply a considerable part, but I would rather have more than less—If you would send down half a dozen good Hogs just killed, I should glad & two or three firkins of good Butter—

Chamberlain, from Hunterdon County, was a Colonel in the New Jersey Militia.

To Joshua Loring

Sir,   Baskinridge [N.J.] Jan^ry 19 1778

I had the Pleasure of writing to you on the 29th. Dec^r, which is yet without an Answer—I now enclose the Paroles of Capt. Snyder & others which you sent me with the Exchange of 24 Novr. last & for which I am ordered again to ask Capt. Vandyke & others mentioned in the Exchange I sent you of Novr. 20th.—I hope you cannot still have objections to this request as the officers demand^d. are entitled to Exchange in point of Time and those who have gone to you tho' belonging to the Northern department, yet were considered by us as within the Agreement made between our two Generals as Commanders in Chief of the whole forces on each side of the Question—*I confess that Capt. Gamble was not entitled to his Exchange according to the Time of his Capture, neither can I ask it in that point of View, but then he must be considered as having broke his Parole by not complying with the Terms of it*—I must beg the fav^r. of your acquainting D^r. Sandon that it is expected that he should discharge the moneys advanced for him by Capt. Patterson before his Exchange is perfected—

I find by a late Exchange, that Capt. Keeting of the new Levies, has been sent in from Connecticut for Capt. Trowbridge & a Lieutenant for M^r. Callender—I was much surprised at hearing that Capt. Trowbridge was a Prisoner, as by my Books it appears that Capt Francis was sent in for him, last Winter—And it must have been by mistake that a Lieutenant was sent in for M^r. Callender who was only a Cadet in our Service— perhaps you may explain this matter which at present I do not understand

I have ordered all the Officers (Prisoners) from the Westward, and have sent in to M^r. Ferguson at Philadelphia ye proposed Exchange on Parole for the whole in our Custody, but have not yet rec^d. an Answer This I promised to send you, but hearing you were on your Way for Philadelphia, I conclude you must have seen it there—
   I am informed that my last Letter to M^r. Pintard of the 29 Utmo was not delivered to him—I should be glad to know what part of it gave offence, that I may take my future Measures accordingly—I am also instructed to ask the reasons of confining a number of our Officers in your Provost. *Particularly* Major Pierce Capt. Van Dyke Capt. Flahaven, and many others you must be well acquaited with, being closely Confined in your Provost—This request is designed to prevent retaliation taking Place, in Case these Gentlemen are suffering for any undue behavior of which they have been regularly convicted—
   I must beg the favour of being informed, if the Jenifer Pacquet, Capt Hammond from France & who sailed last January, has ben taken by any of your Ships of War or Privateers—On board of this [ship] a Mr Nathan Rumsey was Passenger, whose Friends are extremely desirous of hearing of him—
   As the reports of the distresses & wants of our Prisoners are daily increasing, I am ordered to ask Permission for going into New York to endeavour to put them on a more Comfortable footing—as far as shall be admitted by you—I have wrote to his Exc^y *Sir Henry* Genl. Clinton on this Subject, but if I should be refused this request, I must beg the favour of your obtaining Liberty for M^r. Pintard to come here, in order to settle his Accounts with me—*I shall take Care that Passposts for his coming & returning shall be left for him at Eliz. Town—*
   I have lately seen M^{rs}. Swoope *wife of Coll Swoope* who claims a Promise she alledges you made her some time since of suffering her Husband to return home on Parole—If the proposed Exchange does not take Place, I shall be much obliged by your Influence to obtain this Indulgence for Coll Swoope.

To Henry Clinton

Sir,   Eliz. Town [N.J.] Jan^{ry} 20 1778
   I have the honor of addressing your Excellency by the orders of the Commander in Chief *his Excellency George Washington*, who being

informed of the distresses & wants of the Prisoners of War in New York & Long Island is desirous of having them relieved if possible, and therefore has desired me to ask Permission to visit the Prisoners in New York & *Long Island,* and to *endeavour to* make such Provision for them as shall be in my Power, *and* consistant with you Orders—I also wish, at the same time, to settle my Accounts with M^r. Pintard, shall therefore beg the favour of your Passport for this Purpose under such restrictions as you may think proper to grant it, *assuring you on my Honor that no improper Use shall be made of the Indulgence*—

If this request should be thought inadvisable I must beg the favour, that M^r. Pintard may be allowed to come over here for the above Purpose, and I will be answerable for his safe return—

I have the Honor to be, with due Respect Your Exc^y &

Lieutenant General Clinton commanded British forces in and around New York City.

To Lewis Pintard

Dr Sir,   Baskinridge [N.J.] Jan^{ry} 19th. 1778
Your fav^r. by Major Williams I have duly rec^d. and you may be assured that I am doing every Thing in my Power to hasten you Supplies for our Prisoners—I hope you will soon receive a Boat load of flour from Middle Town Point, and a greater Quantity from Eliz. Town

I have [ ] Days ago ordered some down the North River also, but am afraid it has been delayed by the Ice—You shall have a Supply of wood if possible but this can only be for the Prisoners of War as I take no Charge of any others—I approve of the appointment of other Nurses, *if it should be necessary,* when you are in Cash, should have no Objection to an extraordinary Physician, when you think it really advantageous to those poor fellows—I am sorry any thing in my Letter of the 29th. Utmo from the Valley Forge, should have prevented its delivery which I find has been the Case—I shall send you in, some fresh Beef with the first Boat for present use, till I can give proper directions for sending it in by Way of Kingsbridge unless you think, it will answer in Quarters, which I think might do while the cold weather lasts—I shall not leave Jersey till you are fully supplied, and I hope the delay has not been greatly to your disadvantage—

I have asked Liberty to visit our prisoners with you but if this is refused, then that you may be allowed to come here, in order to settle the

Accounts of your disbursement, for which Purpose you must bring all your Vouchers—If you obtain this Liberty, come to Eliz. Town, where I will take Care that you shall be properly received, and will be answerable for your safe return—

I send the following Sums of money—for Major W^m. Bailey £10:10:0 & 2 ½ Jos. 3 Guineas—5 Pistoles—1/8 Jos. 14 Dollars—Lt Robt. Wilkins £10:10:0 & a Bundle of Cloaths—Lt Danl. Broadhead 1½ Jos. 2 Guineas—& 4 Dollars—L^t. Walter Finney 9 Guineas—1½ Jos. 3 Dollars—D^r. Fullerton 20 Dollars L^t. Rezin Davis 3½ Jos 2 & 5/8 Dolls 3 E. Shill.

To Thomas Bradford

Sir,   New Ark [N.J.] Jan^ry 21 1778

Being in Business here, and an Opportunity offering I improve it to acknowledge the rec^t. of yours by Dr Wiggins, but cannot find out that any Post is established thro' this part of the Country—If any thing material turns up, you must insist on Coll. Lutterloo's finding you an Express, unless you can hire one yourself—Do not fail on rec^t. hereof, to send into Philadelphia 12 or 15 Head of good fat Cattle, and let the Commissary of Issues know, that we must supply our Prisoners there, weekly with Provision to the amount of 600 Men—They are to be fed altogether by us in the future, therefore the utmost attention must be paid to a Constant & unfailing Supply—You had best apply to Coll Harrison at Head Quarters & know if any Thing has happened since I left you, to alter this measure— our Prisoners in New York are in such distress, that I cannot leave this part of the Country till they are supplyed—I shall return to Baskinridge to morrow—Pray remember that you do not neglect to keep Mr Franklin constantly supplyed with Meat, sufficient for the Prisoners Consumption—He has flour enough—

Am &

On January 17, 1778, Washington announced in General Orders that Bradford had been appointed Deputy Commissary General of Prisoners with the Army.

To John Adam

Sir,   New Ark [N.J.] Jan^ry 21 1778
 I wrote you lately, but lest it should not reach you must beg you will
exert yourself to send into New York as soon as the river opens, at least
500 Barrells of Flour, especially when ever the price is regulated—You
may agree to give whatever shall be settled at Hartford or whatever the
Commissary gives—Call on the Commissary to supply you if in his
Power—I hope you will hasten the matter as fast as possible, and add to
the flour a Boat load or two of good hickory Wood—If you fail of flour
with you, endeavour to send it down the East River from Norwalk—Send
in also immediately about 20 Head of Cattle (let them be fat & large) by
the way of Kingsbridge—Let me hear from you by the first Opportunity,
directed to Baskinridge—By the first Opportunity write to D Hale at
Albany, desiring him to forward immediately, the returns of the Hessians
& the Hospital under his Care, and any other Prisoners he may have—

To John Campbell or Commanding Officer on Staten Island

Sir,   Eliz Town Jan^ry 23^d. 1778
 I take the liberty to acquaint you, that expecting a Quantity of flour,
Beef & wood, down to this Place for the use of our Prisoners, agreeable
to the Permission given by Genl Howe, and finding that some Confusion
has lately happened by the Boatman's changing the Sloop that had been
used in this Business, in order to prevent it for the future I have ordered
the Provision & other necessaries from this Place & New Ark to be
transported in the Sloop Plenty, which the Bearer now Commands, and
must beg the favour of your allowing her to pass & repass, under the usual
restrictions, assuring you Sir, that she should not be used for any other
Business, nor the Indulgence abused—
 I had hoped from enlarged Sentiments on the Subject of making
Prisoners of the Inhabitants, that those taken by the late Coll. Dongan
from Woodbridge, would e'er this have been returned to their families, in
Exchange for a greater number, I returned to Staten Island—I doubt not
Sir, when you know that there are several of these Inhabitants still
detained, you will interest yourself in their release—I have wrote to M^r
Loring some time past on this Head, who promised to enquire into the

Matter—
  I have the honor to be &

To Lewis Pintard

Dr Sir,   Eliz Town [N.J.] Jan^{ry} 23^d. 1778
  Herewith you will receive 40 Quarters of Beef w^h. I hope will be a seasonable relief to our Prisoners—I could wish to have a return of them, that I may know how to supply them—I hope that this will be good and whilst the Cold weather lasts, equally serviceable, as if Cattle had been sent in alive—I send these now, as the flour is coming down, but a full load will not be ready before the return of the Boat—

To Archibald Campbell

Sir   Baskinridge New Jersey Jan^{ry} 27 1778
  Your favour without a Date, was received the 8th. Ins^t. and the next Day, the enclosed Letter to Genl. Howe was sent into Philadelphia by a flag of Truce—I should have acknowledge the rec^t. of it before now, but have been waiting an answer from Genl Howe in hopes that I might have been the means of conveying the agreeable news of his concurrance to the proposed Exchange; but in short Sir the same fatality attends it, that does every proposition of the like kind that has been made since I have been in Office—no Answer can be had till much more Time elapses, as would serve for a negotiation for preliminaries of Peace between two crowned Heads—As soon as an Answer does arrive, shall forward it on to you— As every Thing that tends to mitigate the Horrors of War, or to soften the Sufferings of the unfortunate, gives me very peculiar Pleasure, you may depend on my endeavours to obtain Compliance with your request by improving my first arrival in Camp, in an Application to his Exc^y Genl Washington on your Acc^t. and will also write to the Board of War, whose Concurrance from some particular Circumstances I suppose it will be necessary—
  I expect to be in Camp by the middle of February, and if I can accomplish your desires my humanity will be highly gratified—
    Am &

Lieutenant Colonel Archibald Campbell, of the Seventy-First Regiment of Foot, was a prisoner of war at Concord, Massachusetts.

To Lewis Pintard

Sir,   N York [New York City] Feb^ry 9 1778
    I am much distressed to find the Imprudance of our officers in running me to so enormous an Expence for mere Ornaments, that can add nothing to their real Comfort—The difficulty I have met with & many more I still meet with to find them bare necessaries, obliges me to direct you not to allow any farther Orders for Ornaments, but to confine yourself to plain regimental Cloathing & real necessaries, without either Lace or Epaulets till the present enormous Debt for Clothing & Board is first discharged
    Am &

To Robert Livingston

Sir,   New Jersey Feb^ry 21 1778
    I am under a necessity of sending into New York several Sloop loads of Wheat: this cannot be done with any Convenience at any other Place as well as by North River—I have there fore directed the Bearer one of my deputies, to wait on you, to know it you will contract to furnish me with any Quantity under Twenty Thousand Bushells, at the regulated Price, be it what it will, to be forwarded down to New York immediately on the opening of the River—I do not mean that it should go all at once, but as fast as possible—It is for the use of our unhappy Prisoners in that City, whose Cries can no longer be unheard—If you think of undertaking any part of it, I must beg you will not loose a Moments Time in setting about it, as it will not admit of delay—You may also engage for the Transportation of it, if you please, and I will furnish Passports for the Purpose—If you should not choose to undertake this Business, pray advise M^r. Adam how to proceed, at the same Time, I must beg you will not mention the matter to any Person whatever, as it may injure him in perfecting the Contract—
    Am Sir &

Livingston was a wealthy landowner and political leader in New York.

To John Nicoll/Nicholls

D^r. Sir   New Jersey Feb^{ry} 21 1778
I am happy in having an Opportunity of asking how you do in these troublesome Times—I have directed the Bearer Mr John Adam one of my deputies to call on you to assist him in the Purchase of a Quantity of wheat for the use of our unhappy Prisoners in the City—Pray do all you can do, as it is much wanted—My best Compliments to Mrs Nicholls—Let Coll. Allisons family & Coll McGlohary's know that I see them both well a few days past—
Am &

John Nicoll or Nicholls was at New Windsor, New York.

To John Adam

Sir,   Baskinridge [N.J.] Feb^{ry}. 21 1778
You will please immediately to proceed to the North River & there endeavour to purchase any Quantity of wheat under 20000 Bushells, which I beg you will hasten down the River to Mr Pintard for the use of the Prisoners of War, as fast as possible—
You may engage the Cash or loan office Certificates as soon as I can possibly send them to you—
As soon as possible send into New York Ensign Adamson lately taken Prisoner, having just exchanged him for Ensign Barnitz—If he is not in the State of New York, pray send an Order for this Purpose after him, wherever he is, and if an Opportunity offers let it be sent by Express—
Am &
P.S. Call on the Governor & Gen^{ls} for any assistance you may want

To Joshua Mersereau

D^r. Sir,   Baskinridge [N.J.] Feb^{ry} 21 1778
I cannot say a word at present, more than to desire you will be pleased to make enquiry for the Capt of the Ship Lady Gage, taken lately by the Cumberland Capt. Collins & carried into Falmouth Casco Bay—His Name is Joseph Royal Loring—When you find him, please to send him into New Port Rhode Island, I having Exchanged him with the

Commissary in New York. Let your Enquiry be made immediately, and if you are at any Expence in sending Express after him, if he does not pay it to you, let me have an Account of it & I will pay it—I expect to exchange Coll Campbell in a few days, if he chooses to come this way, you may take his Parole & let him come on to Morris Town in Company with the first genteel officer that is coming this way—when he gets there, he must remain till he acquaints me with the arrival, unless he meets a Lr from me—If Coll Campbell chooses to go into New Port, and will wait a few days, he shall hear from me again.

Am &

To Azariah Dunham

Sir,   Baskinridge [N.J.] Feb^{ry} 23^d 1778

I expected to see you, but being ordered off immediately to Camp, and obliged to desire you to give orders that Mr Sears may receive about three or four Cattle once in about Ten days untill I return—I was extremely sorry to find that you prevented Mr Sears from taking such Cattle as he thought would do—when I got to New York, I was ashamed of those you sent, they being scarcely fit to Eat—I have ordered three of them to be returned to Turkey, as absolutely injurious to the Service to send, and directly contrary to my orders—I could wish you would consider the good of the Cause in general & not ruin the public Credit, by an ill timed Parsimony—

Am Sir your Hble Servt

Dunham was Assistant Commissary of Purchases at Morristown, New Jersey.

To Thomas Peters

D^r. Sir,   Camp [Valley Forge] March 2^d. 1778

Last Evening I returned here from a tedious fatiguing & dangerous Journey from New York—I find myself so hurried, notwithstanding my being almost wearied out, that I have but a Moment to acknowledge the rec^t of yours of the 3^d of Feb^{ry} being the only one rec^d from you since I left York Town—I shall carefully attend to Govr. Henry's letter, altho' I have already exchanged Cap Traverse—I do not forward on D^r. Me[nzie]s Letter, as he has been already exchanged by me at New York, and therefore beg you will forward him on here as fast as possible—He must clear off all scores with you before he sets off—If he wants money let him have it on my Acc^t. transmitting me by him, an Acc^t. of what he receives— Let him come no farther in Camp than my Quarters which is 4 Miles from Head Quarters on the road from Reading—He must enquire for the Clothier's Store as I lodge in the same House—I could wish he was sent in Company with some genteel Officer coming this way—

Be pleased to return to Lancaster the latter end of the next week or begin of W after all the Prisoners (Officers & Privates) excepting Mr Conolly with you, the Officers first discharging all their Arrears, and giving the necessary Paroles to come on to Lancaster & from thence to such Places as they shall be ordered *as I expect to send them in immediately to Philadephia in the General Exchange—I must beg you will prepar to receive the Prisoners as they come from the west ward*

I have sent on Mr Connolly's Letter, and shall do all in my Power to finish the Exchange I have already begun for Coll Swoope, he having been sent from New York on my Application before I knew that I should go in myself—

As to the Officers in Confinement at Carlisle, I wish you to inform them that they are now kept confined for the like number of our Officers who are in the Provost of New York, and that they shall be confined no longer than those officers—Any remonstrance they think proper to make to Genl Howe on this occasion, shall be transmitted to him.—Matters are so changed, and now in so good a Train, that for the present, I think it best to defer doing any Thing on the late resolution of Congress—I have never heard of any allowance for taking up british Prisoners, but have only paid the real Labour and Expence spent on the Occasion, lest it should tempt them to desert merely for the sake of getting a Premium, given to some friend to be divided between them—

To Henry Hugh Fergusson

Sir,   Camp [Valley Forge] March 2^d 1778

Being just returned from Jersey & New York, I am obliged in a hurry to enclose a Letter to Genl Howe from Mr Commissary Loring, who is sollicitious to have an Answer sent out to me immediately, that it may be forwarded to him—The extreme badness of the Roads & the Ice in the Rivers, have lengthened my Journey to a fortnight, which is the reason of

Genl. Howe's not receiving it sooner—I have it in command from his Ex^y the Commander in Chief to mention the Case of Major Genl Lee; he being ordered *by General Howe* in a Man of War to Philadelphia from New York—Genl. Lee objects to such a Voyage at this Season of the Year, and earnestly sollicits permission to come on by Land, in such route as shall be prescribed—He can come in Company with M^r. Loring or *Major Williams* any other Officer that may be thought proper. Major Genl Prescott, with several other Officers have been arrived at New York for many weeks past, but no Instructions have been rec^d relative to the late Agreement for admitting Officers on Parole, or Information of its Existence—*In behalf of* I must beg you will apply to Genl Howe on this Occasion & obtain the necessary order in fav^r. of Genl Lee, in whose behalf and that of Mr Loring I must beg an immediate Answer—I expect your Officers in from Virginia as soon as possible—

    Am &

March 7th. 1778—Wrote to Govr. Henry of Virginia to send in Capt Goodrich for Capt Traverse, as I had exchanged them & given a written Promise to return him immediately—

    sent it by Major Jamison to Cap Traverse to forward—

To William Atlee

My Dr Sir,   Camp March 4 [Valley Forge] 1778

    I take the earliest Opportunity on my arrival from New York of congratulating you on your Brothers return & answering yours of the 15 Jan^{ry} rec^d. here since my departure—If you have any Money in your hands to forward to me for the use of the Prisoners, pray pay for the flour sent me, if not let me know how I should forward you the amount, which you sent & acquaint me with the Carting &—I am sorry you are so crowded with the Prisoners, but as a General Exchange is just taking Place, I must beg that you will not send forward any more, but rather prepare for receiving those from the westward on their way to the City, but you shall be first relieved of those you have, except a few from York Town, who may perhaps Come on first—pray write to Coll Haller not to send one on to Lancaster

In order to accommodate the sick and wounded, I beg you will establish an Hospital & appoint proper Surgeons, Nurses & & under your own directions—D[r] Shippen will give you general directions for the government of it, if you think them necessary—If you are successfull in taking the Villains who have taken off the Hessians, pray have them prosecuted by the Civill Law & give them their deserts [sic]—Be so kind as to prepare about 250 of the Hessian Prisoners to come off on the first order—By this Exchange Lebanon will be evacuated in favor of the Laboratory—I duty rec[d] yours enclosing the Cash for Major Galbreath—Be so kind, if you can them find out, as to send down to me a John Hamilton of the 49th Reg[t] servant to Ca[pt] Smith James Davis a servant to Maj[r] Crew & [writer's blank] Falls servt to Maj[r] Leslie—Direct them to call at my Quarters on the Reading Road near Gordons ford—I could wish to have them put under the care of some party coming this way—There is a Peter Slightly a hessian—to send to Gen[l] Washington Plantation

To Henry Haller

D[r] Sir,   Camp Valley Forge March 4 1778.
    You will be pleased not to send forward any Prisoners now with you, as I expect to send for those you have, to be returned to Philadelphia without delay as a general Exchange is now to take place—The Officers are likewise to settle their Accounts & keep themselves in readiness to come off as soon as possible.

To Henry Hugh Fergusson

Sir,   Camp [Valley Forge] March 6 1778
    I have this Morning been favoured with your several Letters of the 6th. 30 & 31 Jan[ry] which came to Camp during my Absence to the Eastward—It would have given me Pleasure to have had it in my Power to oblige you by any little Civilities I could have paid to M[rs]. Tomlinson, who I hope has safely arrived eer this—I am obliged to you for the returns of our Prisoners and will forward those of yours lately come in from the Bay as soon as I can get them drawn off—
    The money has been rec[d]. & sent to M[r] Knoblock—He has long since wrote in to have an Acknowledgement of his being a Com[d]. Officer & of

what rank, but has not rec^d any Answer, which has prevented so great an Indulgence to him as otherwise would be allowed—If he is a *commissioned* Officer I could wish for his Sake, it was made known—I have this day wrote to *several of* my deputys to forward the three Servants you mention to my Quarters, to be sent in to you according to your desire, and shall be glad at any Time to comply with any request of this Nature—If your think proper you may send out for them when they arrive, the drivers of the Cattle lately taken in Bucks County Mr Saml Dunham Senr & Ju^r & Mr James Dunham the old Man has a family who may suffer by his Absence and is one of my Jersey Neighbours—I forward from his family two half Jos. a piece for them, which I will be obliged by your delivery, also a Bundle wrapt in a Blankett.—I have not heard of Mr Cavennaugh neither do I know any of the Circumstances of the Exchange you refer to—On your informing me of by whom made or sending a Copy of his Parole, I will enquire into the matter immediately—I expect my Baggage will Come here in a day or two when I will send the Names of the Persons for whom the Bundles were sent, in by Mr Clymer, my Papers being with my Baggage *not having yet got into Camp*—

To Thomas Franklin

Dr Sir,   Camp [Valley Forge] March 6 1778
     On my Arrival here, your Letter of the 14 Feb^{ry} was put into my Hands, acknowledging the rec^t of the Cattle & flour—I was very sorry to find by your Certificate *sent to Genl Washington by Genl Howe* as well as by the Letter, that the least suspicion should have arose that we ever thought our Prisoners not being attend to by Mr Ferguson & yourself—So far from it, that since Mr Fergusons appointment, every Account we have rec^d. as well as my own Knowledge of you both as Men of Humanity & Virtue have given us the fullest Satisfaction that every prudent means in your Power has been used for their relief; would to God it had been thus from the beginning of this unhappy dispute, many altercations & hard Thoughts as well Deaths would have been prevented—
     The uneasiness that arose and the accounts transmitted to Congress were done while we [lay] at White marsh before your appointment—If you are now at liberty to purchase necessarys for the Prisoners, in the same manner as allowed at New York, I beg that they may want for nothing that will add to make their Captivity tolerable—If the permission

you rec^d extended no further, then the quantity you mention in your Letter I will exert myself to send in what I can from Lancaster—

I should be glad to know if you have rec^d any Supply of Vegetables & of Wood yet from my Agents down the river, and when you will want any more flour or Beef & what Quantity—

Am

To Joshua Loring

Sir,   Camp Valley Forge March 8 1778

You will undoubtedly think it strange that you have not heard from me e'er this—I found the Roads almost impassable, so that I was a complete fortnight in getting to the camp from your City, having stopped only two days at Home—

As soon as I arrived I obtained Genl Washingtons Permission for your coming by Land, and sent off your Letter to Genl. Howe but did not receive an Answer till late this Morning—Enclosed you have the Answer & a Passport for coming on to Philadelphia—I was in great Hopes to have waited on you myself through Jersey, but I am so circumstanced, from the State of the general Exchange, as to render it impracticable at present, and indeed the roads are so extreme bad, as to make it almost an Herculian Labour—I am afraid you will be put to difficulty for good Horses at South Amboy, and therefore think you had best bring them over, altho' Genl Lee's being with you, will obtain all the assistance the Country can afford—

I am sorry that there has been a little Altercation between our two Generals during my Absence, arising from some unlikely Accidents, that I could wish had not happened—However I found a General Exchange agreed upon, and Commissaries appointed to meet next Tuesday for settling matters in difference, so that I hope you will find all Matters settled and the Exchange in forwardness—

I should be glad of a Line as soon as possible, giving me a rough Estimate of the sum yet due, to the Landlords for the Officers Board on Long Island, with an arrearaged account how long they have laid out of their Money, or whether they have ever rec^d. any part—I am in hopes all the Acc^{ts}. will now be amicably adjusted that matters may go on more smoothly in future—I have wrote to the Eastward about your Brother, and have directed the forwarding on the several Officers agreeable to my

Promise—I expect Coll. Campbell every day at Morris Town, but am prohibited from sending him into the City till Coll Allen is sent out in Exchange for him—This I imagine arises from Genl. Lee's being so long detained after Genl. Prescotts arrival—I wish they could both meet at E. Town Point—Be so kind as to let me hear of your arrival at Philadelphia—

Copy of Passport
March 8 1778
Joshua Loring Esqr & Major Griffiths Williams Officers in the Service of the King of Great Brittain have his Excellency *the Commander in Chief* Genl Washingtons Leave to pass in Company with the Honble. Major Gen: Lee through New Jersey, to the City of Philadelphia, taking their Route from Brunswick to Cranberry & thro' Borden Town & Burlington from whence they may either go by water down the river or cross over to Bristol & then go down the usual Road to Philadelphia—And all American Officers are hereby desired to aid & assist them accordingly to be in force one Month

To Charles Lee

Dr Sir   Camp Valley Forge March 8 1778
Immediately on my arrival here, which was not till two weeks after my leaving you, occasioned by the Ice & most dangerous Roads you ever saw, I sent in to Philadelphia to obtain the necessary directions from Genl. Howe, for your coming thro Jersey, This I did not obtain till this Morning, which will be a sufficient Apology for the unexpected delay in hearing from me—
I have enclosed Genl. Howe's Letter to M^r. Loring, who is to accompany you, and if Major Williams thinks proper to take a Jaunt of Pleasure at this Season of the Year, he has liberty to make the third man— The Route presented is much in your favour on Account of the Roads, which are but one degree from being impassible, by the middle Road thro' Princeton & Trenton; it is therefore fixed for your landing from Staten Island, either at Amboy or South Amboy, which last will be the best— from either of these Places thro' Cranberry & Borden Town & Burlington, from whence you can either go down the River by water, or cross to Bristol & go down the usual Road by Land at your Pleasure—I wished &

expected to have been added to your Company but my Business is accidentally such as to render it impracticable—

Be so good as to let me hear of your passing from Bristol or wherever meet with any of our out Posts—The General expects that you will not be delayed in Philadelphia, but that he will have the pleasure of seeing you, soon after your Arrival there—

P.S. If it is equal to you, I should think you would save trouble, either by landing at Amboy or going quite up to Brunswick if the wind is fair; but lest that should not be the Case, I have wrote to the Com. Officer at Eliz. Town who will aid you as much as possible—

To Lewis Pintard

Dr Sir,   Camp [Valley Forge] March 8 1778
        After one of the most terrible Journeys you ever knew, I arrived here in a fortnight after leaving you—Two Days & an half were used in getting to Eliz Town Point, and I was very near being finally lost—We parted our Anchor and Cable & had to break thro' a quarter of a Mile of thick Ice—I found expresses waiting for me at home; therefore could not delay to put any Thing in order—
        I had only Time to give a few Orders for forwarding Wheat from the North River & flour from Brunswick to keep you going till I could return, which I hope will be punctually obeyed—
        Matters are going on very well here with regard to the Prisoners and I hope will turn out in the end to mutual Advantage—I could wish for an Estimate of the Sums of money yet due for Board on Long Island to the Landlords themselves exclusive of what has been paid them either by Genl. Howe or Genl Robertson, and the Time they have laid out of it on an average—I enclose two half Jos. & a Letter for M^r. John Rolston.—

To Sylvanus Seely

Sir,   Camp Valley Forge March 8 1778
        The Enclosed Letter for Joshua Loring Esqr. I must beg you will forward immediately by a flag to Staten Island—It contains his Exc^{ys} Passport for Genl. Lee coming through Jersey to Philadelphia, in company

with two british Officers—If they land at Eliz. Town you will be please to shew them all the politeness in your Power and assist them on as fast as possible—I thought it best to give you timely Notice of it that—you may have matters ordered accordingly—

As the Gent[n] are all strangers at Eliz. Town you will please to provide proper lodgings for them if they stay with you a Night

Seely, a Colonel in the New Jersey Militia, was then at Elizabeth Town, New Jersey.

To Horatio Gates

Sir,   Camp Valley forge March 10th 1778
My being absent from Camp (at New York) ever since the setting of your Board, has occasioned your not having heard from me relative to my department—I duly rec[d]. your favour of the 2[d]. Ins[t]. and can assure you that it is not on the present Occasion that my uneasiness has first arose respecting the Improper Situation of the Prisoners of War—This has been the subject of my remonstrances from the first of my Appointment, and indeed it was the Terms I insisted on the first Time of my being at the Board of War, that I should have proper Places built for the purpose of keeping Prisoners together, as I could not undertake to be answerable for till such Places were put into my Power—Had my repeated Requests been attended to on this Head I could by this Time, have received them all, but the Board of War have themselves only to blame for every inconvenience attending the present State of the Prisoners—I need not mention Sir, that I do not refer to the present Members, who have so lately taken their Seats—On an Application on this Subject, some time the Month of June last, I rather thought myself so casually treated, that I have been silent ever since, till I was last at York Town—At Present Sir I can only lament with you, the losses we are daily sustainng in the flight of Prisoners, not only from Lancaster but also from New England States where is it much worse—What can we expect from 4000 Prisoners, scattered throughout the Country in private Houses without any Guard or overseer. The Hessians are let out to Work in different parts of the Country by express orders of the board of War—I have done every Thing in my Power for the two past Months to endeavour to secure those under my Care; I have hired a large Ship for this purpose (at a high rate) in Connecticut, which is fitting up to receive those in that State, altho' I have my fears & doubts of their safety even there, as a parcell of armed Boats, with a landing of land

forces at the same Time might prove dangerous. Mr Attlee lately wrote me of those Hessians being taken off, and that he was in pursuit of the Agents in this Business, which is all I have heard of it—You may depend on it, that the first Prisoners who go in, shall be those most exposed; in the mean Time, I know of no possibility of obtaining Places of Security for them; as I am clearly of Opinion, that the further they are back in the Country the more danger from them—

As to my waiting on the Board, it will be impossible for me to do it for some weeks, nor could I have done it before Consistent with the Service, had they previously have acquainted me with their desire, which your Letter was the first Intimation of—I am so engaged that I have scarcely time to write a Letter—The increasing demand ag^t. me for the support of our Prisoners in New York & Philadelphia, wrecks my Invention to find means of Answering—I am now in advance & in debt upwards of fifteen Thousand Pounds, besides the old Board of the Officers on long Island which is £7000 more—To answer this I have never yet rec^d. from Congress but 10000 Dollars—I must beg that the Board will return me by the Bearer 20 or 25000 Dollars on Acc^t. of my department—The greatest Part of it may be in loan Office Certificates, of 1000 Dollars & under.

I must also beg that I may have orders on the Loan offices of Massachusets & Connecticut for 4000 Dollars each, as my deputies there have not had a farthing for the last twelve month—

I have fully considered the Scheme of retaliation on the Officers in general, *with the Assistance of a number of Officers* here, but can assure you, it will on experiment be found a most impracticable Business, untill we get Places of Confinement ready, and Guards who can be depended on, and who may be punished for neglect of Duty—The Militia Guards are rather worse than none, except in name—

As Matters now stand here; it is the Opinion of the Committee from Congress, and the General has given in to it for the present, that the Officers from the Westward should be delayed for a short Time, wherefore I shall write to M^r. Peters and M^r. Attlee to make Provision for them in some of the small Towns, till we can determine what to do—I shall forward to Philadelphia those come to Lancaster, and make a demand of the like number now in the Provost of New York, and wait the Issue, before any more are sent in—I expect Coll Campbell from Boston, will soon arrive at Morris Town, agreeable to my orders for that purpose—I have wrote to Mr Loring that if Lt Coll. Ethan Allen, meets him at Eliz. Town Point, he may be Exchanged but that I am prohibited from sending him in till Allen comes out—I had the pleasure of exchanging about a dozen Officers & as many Privates the old in Captivity, who I brought out with me; this was done principally with Officers who had been sent in last Winter & not accounted for by the Enemy—I enclose a Copy of the Substance of my report to Genl Washington on my return from New York. I am so extremely hurried that I could not possibly copy it at large with the Papers referred to in the Original—Also a Copy of a Letter rec^d yesterday from M^r. Ferguson—We know not here, of any mention made to Genl. Howe of the Exchange of Govr Franklin, and are Convinced that no proposal of this kind can be attended to without Consulting the State of Jersey—and even then I believe they would be glad to give a Brig^r. Genl. for him—but as to Mr Connolly, I am of opinion he ought to be forwarded on immediately while Genl. Howe is in the humor of it—I long to hear of the finishing of fort Frederick as I really believe it will have a greater Effect on the Treatm^t of our Prisoners, than 20 remonstrances—

PS. As the State of Jersey expects my attendance at Congress, it will be necessary to appoint some Person to take my department—If he was to be with me a fortnight before I leave the Office it might be to his advantage—I know of no Person within my Knowledge who would fill it better than Wm Attlee Esqr of Lancaster if he will but accept it—

Major General Gates was then President of the Board of War, which was meeting at York, Pennsylvania.

To William Govat

Sir,   Camp V F [Valley Forge] March 10, 1778
        I received your favour on my return from New York and must beg your will take the Trouble of forwarding the Bills of Exchange mentioned therein to me, directed to be left at Head Quarters or at my own lodgings, and I will take Care that they are negotiated so as not to risque any Loss to the publick from any Damages, in Case of Protests—Please to let me know if that are taken for the two Dollars p^r week allowance to Officers or not—

To Thomas Peters

D[r] Sir,   Camp V F [Valley Forge] March 11th 1778
    By accounts rec[d]. from the Board of War & from M[r]. Attlee I find
that the Officers from Virginia are coming on—I did not think they could
have been so forward these dreadfull roads—They were designed to be
immediately sent in to Philadelphia on the Agreement for mutual Paroles
being taken—but as several have been sent in and no returns made or
orders given therefor, it is thought prudent not in send in any more till
Gen[l]. Lee & some others are liberated; wherefore I must beg you will
immediately provide Quarters for them in some of the neighbouring
Towns as Leiditz &c for a few Weeks—I have wrote to the same Effect
to M[r] Attlee, who will inform you of what he can do—I think they had
best be turned aside & not suffered to pass thro' York Town—It will be
expected, that they all produce Receipts or Evidences of all arrears being
paid off, before they go in to Philadelphia—If they put up with the
common country fare, the Inhabitants ought not be allowed to charge
more than two Dollars p[r] week, as this rule is observed with the Enemy—
    Be so good as to send me returns of their rank & Number as they
come on—The Commissioners meet the 31st. Ins[t]. where I hope a General
Exchange will take place—
        Am &

To William Atlee

D[r] Sir,   Camp V F [Valley Forge] March 11 1778
    Your favours of 7th & 8th Ins[t]. are now before me—The horrid State
of the Roads prevented me from expecting the Prisoners from the
Westward so soon—Having sent in several Officers to New York &
Philadelphia on the mutual agreem[t]. of our Generals, but instead of
sending out our officers in their Room, Gen[l] Lee was ordered moved by
Sea to Philadelphia, and afterwards on my remonstrance, by land, and
when I demanded the other's at New York was informed that Gen[l]
Clinton had not rec[d] any Information of the agreem[t]. & therefore could not
liberate them—This has caused some delay to the farther Execution of the
Agreement till Gen[l]. Lee & others are liberated, wherefore I must beg the
favour of you immediately to provide Quarters in some of the little Towns,
for as many of those coming on as you can—If you are hard pushed, you

must send on a few to Reading—I enclose my Letter to Mr Peters for your perusal, & shall be glad you will let me know what you can do—Seal & forward it on with the one to the Board of War as soon as possible—As Capt Battout, Lieut^s. Francis and Wilmot are so far on their way, have enclosed a Passport for their coming on, & going to the City, you will please to call on the Commanding Officer, for some proper Person to take Charge of them to the Enemy's Lines—Also you have herewith a Copy of the Parole they are each to sign, but it is expected that they leave Vouchers with you of all arrears being paid off, and also that L^t. Wilmot did pay off the Enclosed Acc^{ts}—The one for board is a publick one, the other from a private Surgeon employed by him—As to Capt. Carmichael, I believe on the whole you had best send him with Capt Battout, on the same Conditions, if you have no reason to the Contrary—I should be glad of an Acc^t how he has been treated and also the history of the two Sergeants [   ] taken from the flag as there is a little Sparring with the two Gen^{ls}, on their Acc^t.

To Henry Haller

Sir,   Camp [Valley Forge] March 12, 1778
You will please to take the respective Paroles of Capt. Speake, Capt. McCrea & M^r. Knoblock according to his rank, agreeable to the Enclosed Copy, and send them under the Care of some proper Person down thro' white Marsh to Philadelphia—I enclose a Passport for that Purpose, only you will fill up the Blank with the Name of the Person who goes down with them—They must previously produce you vouchers of the Payment off all men for Board &c—You may also take Capt George Fenwicks Parole to go to Philadelphia (at the same time) & to return within two Weeks—I had sent this permission immediately after his leaving Camp, but by some means or other it had been neglected—I find that he has formerly treated our Prisoners with great humanity when he was in New York & therefore deserves a return of favour—I never could get from the Enemy an Acknowledgement of M^r. Knoblock being a commissioned Officer, till last night—

As I expect a number of Officers (Prisoners) on from the Westward every day, I must beg you will provide Quarters for about a dozen of them, which may be sent from Lancaster—If can be only for a short time—I am astonished at the Behaviour of Capt. Nicolls, having never returned to this day—It is such Behaviour & Conduct that injures other Prisoners; I wish you to mention this to Cap^ts Speake & McCrea—Whatever he has left behind you might take Care of, that they are not sent in to him—

    Am &

To George Washington

Sir   Camp [Valley Forge] March 3^d 1778

    Having perused General Howes letter to your Excellency of the 21st February last, a sight of which you was pleased to favour me with, I cannot but regret the necessity I find myself under of taking notice of the following sentence and of course troubling you with this letter—General Howe says "Exclusive of this Persuasion I cannot help observing, that Mr Boudinotts representation of circumstances within my immediate knowledge, has been such, as should prevent my giving much Credit to the Report he has made of those at a greater distance from Explanation"—

    Your Excellency will not wonder, that this ungenteel as well as ungenerous Insinuation against my Veracity, has greatly hurt my finer feelings—General Howe may claim some deferrence from his superior Rank & Station in life, but in point of Integrity and moral Character, I should think myself highly injured in yielding to him in the minuest particle—I may be mistaken, and I may be imposed upon by the misrepresentation of others, but I hope, to retain to the End, that Character of unstained Veracity, which I have hitherto supported—I presume General Howe refers to the State of Facts published by Congress the 21st Jany last and contained in the Report of the Board of War: I am not at all surprized that they have made this impression; but they are of too much importance to be glanced by with so slight a Parry. I am answerable for no more of those Facts, than those collected from my Report—none of them are made on my own knowledge but I am able to support each of them by all the weight of Evidence, that human Testimony (at a remove from self Evident Propositions) is capable of, and that with ten fold Aggravations—Your Excellency will remember that my Report to the Board of War, was prior to the Appointment of Mr Franklin, as our Agent, and about the Time of Mr Fergusons being made Commissary of Prisoners; and related altogether to the Enemys treatment of our Prisoners previous to that appointment, and to our meeting on the lines—But as it will be best to bring this matter to a point, and General Howe seeming to rely principally on one fact, which I suppose is that alluded to as being of his own knowledge, when he says "It is asserted from the evidence conducted by this Gentleman" (meaning myself) "that your officers Prisoners with us, have not had any Allowances for their Subsistance, altho' it is notorious that all the officers who have been boarded in the Country, were for a considerable time allowed two Dollars each p^r week" In answer to this I will premise that our officers have been boarded out, on Long Island, at two Dollars p^r week—That Mr Loring the British Commissary of Prisoners, by his letter to your Excellency of the 24th of March 1777 did declare that "your officers have two Dollars per week allowed them, to pay their Board and Lodging, agreeable to a similar resolve of your Congress to supply our officers when Prisoners with the like Sum &c" But so far from ever having fulfilled this Engagement, if Genl Howe can make it appear that he has ever paid this two Dollars per week in any one Instance to any American Officer admitted to his Parole then I will acknowledge that I have been misinformed and of course have misrepresented this matter—This is a simple Fact, and asserted to be within General Howes own knowledge, and to be so notorious—But if the Contrary of this appears, from the fullest evidence in my Possession, and should appear so to Genl Howe himself upon Examination, I hope he will allow you Excellency in your turn, to judge of the Credit to be given to the other Facts contained in his letter, relative to our treatment of the British Prisoners—The Evidence to set this matter in a clear point of Light, and on which I have founded my representation, and the above Assertions, is as follows—The repeated declarations of every Officer, that has been liberated, as well as those in captivity: many of the first are to be had, and who are ready to make Affadavit of the Fact. The heavy complaints of the inhabitants, on account of their being so long out of their money, alledging their never having received a farthing of the old Board, except in a few Instances, where the Officers have paid it themselves— From the Accounts and receipts of several of the Land lords who were paid, on my leaving New York, for those Officers who were Exchanged and came out with me, in which they charged the Board from the beginning without allowing any Credit From the express declaration of the British Commissary of Prisoners to my Agent in New York, who by his Letter of May 19 1777 says "Mr Loring informs me that his Excellency the General will permit you to send in not only necessary provisions for the

Consumption of the Prisoners, but also as much more to be sold, as will furnish them with every other Necessary, that they may require—but I am desired to inform you, that it will now be expected, that full Supplies be sent in for all the Prisoners now here, and for all such as may hereafter be brought in." And by another letter of the 9th of June following he says "Mr Loring says the Officers Prisoners with you pay their own Board, and that your Officers are therefore to pay theirs, which you ought to provide for without Delay; for it cannot be expected that the inhabitants will keep them well if they are not paid for it" Again by another of the 24th Octr last "The officers taken on Staten Island will be sent over to Long Island provided I will be answerable to pay their Board, but this I cannot do without your directions, as you informed me in a former Letter that the Money you sent out, was not to be applied towards payment of their Board, for that you paid the Board of the British Officers, and that no deduction was to be made until an Exchange took place—However this may be, I would advise you by all means to furnish me with Ways and Means to do it, it will be best on many Accounts and tend to the Comfort and advantage of your Officers—I advised you heretofore to pursue this Method, and told you that the Board of those on Long Island was not paid, the Consequence of which was, an indifference toward them and a disgust in their Land lords, for it cannot be expected, they will use them so well when they are not paid, as they would if they were paid"—All these letters were forwarded open, by the British Commissary who of course knew their contents—From the Acknowledgement of General Robinson and the Commissary when I called on them to know why it was not paid—and the Generals expressly requiring me to provide for the payment of the old Board, alledging that the Inhabitants looked upon him as security for it, having refused to take the Officers from the Prison Ships, on account of the old Arrears not being discharged, until he gave them encouragement, that he would see them paid—From Mr Pintard our Agent at New York, being obliged to become responsible to Genl Robertson for the future Board of the Officers, before they would be allowed to go on the Island, from the Ships, as appears by his letter of the 22^d Decr last "the 10th Instant all the Officers were removed from the ships to Long Island again, where the inhabitants refused to take them in, as their former Board is not paid, and I was informed by Genl Robertson that if I would not engage to pay their Board, he would be obliged to send them on board the Ships again, which I knew would be very disagreeable to them and therefore to prevent it, I have taken upon me to pay it, and it is expected to be done monthly." And on the 15th of January last he adds "The assistance I am obliged to afford to the Prisoners in the Provoost, will also occasion a great Expence, and If I am obliged to pay the former Board of the Officers, which is insisted upon, it will amount to a considerable Sum."

I need make no Comments on these Letters, they speak for themselves and add Weight to the United Testimony of the liberated Prisoners—

As to the Substance of the Conversation with Mr Ferguson, I believe, from his general Character, that he is a Man of Honor and Integrity and therefore should not think of providing Evidence of any Transaction with him, altho' if it was necessary, two Gentlemen Col White and Capt Smith both of the Light Dragoons and a Lady were present and can vouch my Representation; besides which not choosing to trust my Memory, I immediately after, committed the whole that passed between us to Writing, according to my usual Practise—add to this the following Extract from his letter to me of the 28th Nov 1777 immediately on his Appoin^t "the private Soldiers complain much for want of Cloathing—indeed they are in a miserable Situation, many of they being without Breeches, Shirts, Shoes or Stockings—It would be an Act of Humanity to order them a supply of those Necessaries, was it but a partial one, and of the coarsest kind it might be extremely useful, by being distributed to the most necessitous— Coarse woollens are plenty here and a small Sum laid out in that Article would go a great Way in alleviating their suffering" On the 1st of December I met Mr Ferguson on the lines I asked an Explanation of the last Clause, when he informed me that we should certainly have liberty to purchase Cloaths in the City and proposed my appointing an Agent, as I was not to be admitted myself—It was at this time and on this occasion that I nominated Mr Franklin, but at the same time requested Mr Ferguson to call on Genl Howe and get his Approbation of this Allowance—The next day I received a letter from Mr Ferguson of which the following is an Extract "when this is done (meaning the sending out Returns of all their Prisoners in our Hands) "means will be taken to supply our Prisoners with what Necessaries they may want, and permission will be given you to send in Cloathing to yours, but General Howe does not think fit to allow them to be purchased in Philadelphia; neither can he admit your Officers on Parole until the Return before spoke of is transmitted"

The many assurances I have given to your Excellency as well as the Board of War, that since the Appointment of Mr Ferguson and M^r

Franklin to the care of our Prisoners, I was sure that every Justice would be done them, and that the additional Supplys I had enabled Mr Franklin to make, would render them very comfortable, if suffered to provide them with warm Cloathing—This shews the little avail Mr Franklins Certificate can have towards satisfying the Complaint—The difficulty would be to obtain such a Certificate from any man of knowledge in the facts and Veracity (they are both necessary) previous to those Gentlemens appointment—I am confident was it necessary, I could obtain an hundred Addidavits of Men of undoubted Credibility, and the concurrent Testimony of half of the Citizens of Philadelphia (dare they do it) to the Contrary—I have ever done General Howe the Justice, in all my Reports, on this distressing Subject, to insert that it appeared, that he was not privy to the greatest part of the Iniquity, but how far this Ignorance, which might have been prevented, will exculpate him from the Sufferings and Deaths of so many unhappy beings, who fell a sacrifice to the Cruelty of his worthless Servants, is not for me to determine—I know of no indulgence General Howe has shewn to our Prisoners in general that they were not justly intitled to—If their Lives were spared, so were those of the british Prisoners—If there have been a Majority of our Officers admitted to their Paroles, a much greater proportion of british Officers have received the like Indulgence, without first tasting the Sweets of a Provost—If they were fed even with 8 oz or 12 oz of meat & as much bread; the british Prisoners rec^d 16 oz of much better Provisions—If they have been suffered to purchase a Scanty allowance of Cloaths, they paid for it and that in provisions for which the Inhabitants under Genl Howe were starving, and in addition the british Soldiers had the same licence (particularly as to Shoes) in our Country, altho' so scarce an Article—Add to this a Contrast of Treatment of the british Prisoners, to that of our own with the Enemy, from a Comparison of the Bills of Mortality—When the british Prisoners have died one out of Twenty, ours have died Ten out of that number—It is true that our People suffered for want of Cloathing; this also would have been the Case with their Prisoners too, had they, when taken, been stripped almost naked, and marched Miles together bare feet & bare headed in the hottest weather, as is asserted to have been the case with our Prisoners taken on Staten Island, particularly Major Stewart & others, who are ready to make Addidavits of the facts—

I am almost ashamed of the Length of this Letter, but knowing & feeling the necessity of you Exc^{ys} being well informed of a true State of the facts, I have ventured so far on your Patience and would now willingly close it, did not the mention of M^r. Clymer's report not being attended to, call on your Exc^y. for an Answer—Having been refused to visit the Prisoners myself, after the Agreement for that Purpose, I sent in Mr Clymer with some flour & a drove of fat Cattle for the Prisoners, and particularly "for the Purpose of obtaining a faithfull account of the Condition & Treatment of the Prisoners"—He arrived in the City at 4 °Clock in the Afternoon, and an Order was issued by Genl Howe, that he should be out at the Lines, by 5 °Clock the same afternoon. A whole Hour was allowed him to unlade the flour eat his Dinner & obtain this faithfull Acc^t. of the Condition & Treatment of the Prisoners—It is true that the order for his sudden departure being rather delayed (by the Officer who had it in charge) he did not leave the City till 7 °Clock, but the next Morning several miles from the City, was made Prisoner by Genl. Howe's order & brought back with his Horses waggons & attendants, to give an Acc^t. of his delay after the Time limited to him, and for speaking to an Acquaintance by the way, in the presence of the Person under whose Case he was & by his Permission—I know none of these facts, but from Mr Clymers report, which I enclose, altho' your Exc^y has had the Substance of it before—

To enable you Sir, to contribute to Genl Howe's Happiness at the same Time, that it will, in his Opinion, "be to the honor of a Country as once dear to Great Brittain," and which in common Justice ought allways to have been so, I enclose a Testimony, which I humbly hope will be equally conclusive with that of M^r. Franklin's, and fully satisfy the General on this Head—but if it will add to that Satisfaction, I can get the same Evidence from every Quarter, where the Prisoners have been kept—If I have been so happy as to give Satisfaction to your Exc^y by this State of facts, or enabled you in any Degree to convince General Howe of the Injustice of his Complaints, it will add greatly to that Pleasure, with which I have so often expressed myself; with the greatest Respect

Your Exc^ys &

To Robert Lettis Hooper Jr.

Dr Sir,   Camp [Valley Forge] March 16 1778
I am so extremely hurried in preparation for attending the meeting of the Commissioners of Treaty for setting the general Cartel, that I can but acknowledge the rec^t. of your last Letter, and assure you that any little

Services I could do for Capt. Byles gives me great Pleasure—I have been lately informed by a Mr Stephens near Sussex Court House, that there are a few Prisoners of War in that County, and he wrote me to get appointed a Commissary to take Care of them—I am surprized at their being there, and have not the least Idea of any Propriety in suffering them to remain there; must therefore beg you will endeavour to get them to Easton as soon as possible, and the cheapest way you can—

I am grieved at the distresses of my fellow Creatures, tho' my Enemies and the Account you give me of the Prisoners dying so fast since their being curtailed in the Quantity of Provision, gives me much uneasiness— But we have no other way left to relieve our own Brethren in Captivity, but by opening the Enemy's Eyes, by the Sufferings of their own Soldiers; they have been long blind to ours

They laugh at the Idea of 12 oz of Bread & Beef not being enough— Genl Howe says it is quite sufficient—happy indeed had it been for many of our brave Countrymen, had they rec^d two thirds of that Quantity— However altho' I would keep them to that allowance, while in Health, I would nevertheless pay great attention to them while Sick—Give them all the Aid in your Power—Let them have the best Assistance in the Physical department you can get & keep a regular Acc^t. of all Expenditures on this Head—I must beg the favour of you to close all the Acc^{ts}. as Com. of Pris. to the 12th Aprill next when you will set off anew, and I will clear them to that day, as I believe I shall then resign the Office—I wish I knew of some proper Person to recommend to the department who would acept of it—

would not Loan Office Certificates answer for you, as well as Cash it would be much easier for me to send them—

Am &

To Henry Hugh Fergusson

Sir,   Camp V. F. [Valley Forge] March 17th. 1778

In answer to yours of the 6th. Ins^t. relative to L^t. Getting, must inform you that I know nothing more of him, than what I was told by Lt Cameron—when officers undertake to fix upon their own Exchanges, *without consulting the proper Officer*, confusion will allways ensue—If I remember right Lt Gettig undertook to give his Parole that he would get himself Exch^d. for L^t. Cameron, but I never knew a word of it, till I was informed of it lately by M[r]. Cameron. He is not entitled to his Exchange from the time of his Capture, and it would be doing a very essential Injury to him whose right it is, and would involve me in great difficulty, to break thro' this rule I have ever endeavoured to observe—I therefore return the Certificate of his Exchange, and will direct his immediate complying with his Parole—

I have ordered the officers at Lancaster & Reading to be sent immediately into Philadelphia, where they will be arrived e'er you receive this *If I remember right they are Cap[ts]. Batut, Carmichael, M[c]Crea, and Speake, L[ts]. Foster & Wilmot—for whom I must beg you will send out Orders for the release on Parole of Cap[ts]. Vandyke & Whitlock Va[ncurt] Lenox also L[ts]. Skinner & Smock all now confined in the Provost of New York (except Cap[t] Lenox) where they have been for [12] Months on an Average—Major Edminston has also been sent into you some time since, and I expected an order would have been sent eer this for the release of Major Brint[on] Payne (now on long Island) for him—I wish therefore he may be added*—There are also a number arrived in New York from Boston & Connect[t].—I enclose the Names of such of them as I have a Note of together with those sent into you and desire that an Order may be sent out to me, for the release of those whose Names are set ag[t]. them as speedily as possible—I will inquire for M[r]. Weir & exchange him for D[r]. Fullerton on Long Island, as he is most probably to the Eastward, *you had best to mention it in the order you send to New York, and* It will *give directions for bringing* be best to send him into Rhode Island or that City—

Immediately on Rec[t] of yours of the 10th Ins[t]. I wrote a Line to M[rs]. Tomlinson, and send of a rider express to Kennet Square in Search of her, with offers of all the assistance in my Power, but to my great Surprize, he has not yet returned, or have I heard a word from him—so that I fear he is either sick by the way, or taken Prisoner—If I should find M[rs]. Tomlinson, you may depend on my seeing her safe to Philadelphia—I will enquire concerning M[r]. Cavenaugh & let you know the result—two of The Servants mentioned in one of your late Letters are found & coming on, and I hope the other will be with them—

when I know Cap[t]. Anstruther's Serv[ts]. Name he shall be also sent out—Enclosed you have a list of such Bundles sent in, as I can easily find, I hope it will answer to discover the owners of those with you—

I also send herewith, the Return of Prisoners from New York & Massachusets Bay—When I was at New York, I found, for the first

Time, that the Sea & Land Prisoners with you were under separate Commissary's, wherefore in these Returns you will find I have left out all the Sea men—My Ignorance in this respect will apologize for my troubling you with the Seamen in the former list—

Since writing the above, the rider returned from M^{rs}. Tomlinson who informs me she is gone to the City—

I am informed that M^r. Thos. Lowrie a deputy Commissary of Provisions is returned to Philadelphia, having left his family in a distressed Situation, I must beg you will discharge him in Exchange for Commissary M^{ac}Cullogh sent into New York in March last for whom no person has been returned—*I will discharge either Maj. Gordon Pollard or Chrystie [two words illegible] in Massachusets Bay—Mr Loring promised me when in New York to credit me with him*—I enclose a Certificate of his Exchange—I also send by the Flag ½ Jos. ½ Guinea — 9 Dollars — 4 [ ] Doll. 7 Pistareens — 1 Shill. 53 small Pieces For L^t. Robt Woodson—

To John Campbell

Sir,   Camp V F [Valley Forge] March 17th. 1778
Your favour of the 5th. Inst^t. is this Moment handed to me, and as the Express waits shall be obliged to answer you in a hurry—As to the Inhabitants of Woodbridge who are still detained in New York, I know nothing of the Men, only by report, which informs me that they are inoffensive peaceable Inhabitants—indeed from the great Age of some of them, I take it for granted that it must be so thro' necessity— However I verily believe they are full as much so those returned to Staten Island, there having several Charges brought ag^t. them by the violent People among us, to which I did not hearken, but returned them as not being found in arms—

I have given directions for Coll. Campbells meeting me at Morris Town where I expect his arrival daily unless he should choose to delay on acc^t of the roads—I intended to have sent him on immediately to New York, and offered when I was there to exchange him for L^t. Coll Ethan Allen, & to forward him on immediately to New Port or New York—but was refused—This added to the detention of Genl. Lee contrary to the Agreem^t between our two Generals, has caused me to be prohibited sending Coll. Campbell from Morris Town, till Coll

Allen comes out—I have proposed to Mr Loring to meet Coll Allen at Eliz. Town & exchange them there but have had no Answer—
Am Sir &

To Major Dulley

Sir,   Camp V F [Valley Forge] March 17th 1778
I have given Directions that L^t. Coll Campbell of the 71st Reg^t. in the British Service, be permitted to Come from Boston towards Camp, and that he stop at Morris Town till I am acquainted of his Arrival and he hears from me—As he is a gentle man and I could wish to treat him properly, I must desire you will provide him decent Quarters & send off Express to me with the Acc^t. of his Arrival—you may leave word at the Taverns to give you Notice of his Coming and make my Comp^{ts}. to him & let him know that he shall hear from me as soon as possible—

Dulley appears to have been at Morristown, New Jersey.

To William Atlee

D^r. Sir,   Camp V F [Valley Forge] March 17th 1778
Tho scarcely able to set up, am under a necessity of answering yours of the 11 & 13th. Ins^t., together with that of the Officers, which I must do all under one—It allways gives me pleasure to aid or oblige those in distress, but I would willingly do it in such a way as not to bring myself into a Scrape—I know the Situation of the Officers with you, and their Anxiety to get into Philadelphia—I could have wished that they had been stopped at or rather the other side York Town, but this is not their fault, and as it will serve them & ease you, I enclose the Passport they desire, under the same restrictions mentioned before, with the addition of an Attention to the enclosed resolve & Acc^{ts}. w^h are to be first paid in Specie which I forgot to mention before—altho' it was but £6 of Lt Wilmots Acc^t. that was publick monies, but that ought to have been paid in Gold—Before the Gent^n. got down to the White Horse I found out, that they owed ab^t. 200 Dollars for Subsistance at Reading, & that just time enough to stop them at that Tavern—They refused to pay it in Gold or Silver & therefore are

returned back to you, please to send them where you please into the Country, taking a new Parole from them otherwise they must be confined—Capt Carmichael is not in this Number & therefore is gone on—I believe they will not have the Offer again in a hurry—I think you had best send two Officers down with the 17 who are to go when this gets to hand.

Be so good as to forward me the Paroles at your leisure—I am distressed at your not being able to accept my department, as to your Abilities, I will risk my Reputation on them—Indeed I know of no Person who I can venture to recommend besides, but alass your reason is Conclusive, as I know it will be incompatible with that Office—

I will take Care that the money for the flour is transmitted, and as it will save a double Charge, I shall leave the Quarter Master with you to settle the Waggon hire—When I wrote, I was afraid that it fell on you, but if the Quarter Master is to pay it, it will save my getting it again from the one here—As to the Hospital, as soon as I get out I will get Dr Shippen to answer all your Questions—I shall carefully forward the Letters with great Pleasure—Please to send forward the Servants I mentioned & w^h you have found, with the Officers to Philadelphia—

I must heartily congratulate M^rs. Attlee & yourself on the happy occasion of your family—

To Horatio Gates

Sir,   Camp [Valley Forge] March 21st. 1778
Since my last, I rec^d your fav^r of the 9th. Ultmo, where it has been ever since the date I know not—As to the resolves of Congress referred to I new knew any Thing of them till my return from New York, when I found a General Exchange on foot: this in some measure prevents the Execution of them—the Officers being on the move going into the City—I have demanded the Subsistance money from three of them ordered into Philadelphia, in Specie, this they refused to pay, have therefore returned them back to Lancaster, viz. Capt. Battut, L^ts Francis & Wilmot—General Prescot arrived in New York, the latter End of Jan^ry and I should have made a Point of his returning to Connecticut, or Genl Lee's being enlarged, but desisted at the particular & earnest request of Genl Lee, who was apprehensive his Captivity might be lengthened by it—Genl Washington has demanded

Genl Lee without his going into Philadelphia, Gen Howe having sent out a Pass for his going to that City thro Jersey—

I should with pleasure execute the order of Congress as far as it relates to me, as it is a Measure that has been too long neglected, but then the Congress should have remembered that more resolving, was rather injurious to us, when they must have known that it was impossible to be executed—I represented this matter to the Board of War fully, in Decr last, and convinced them that there were not Places of Confinement for above one in five of the Prisoners—I am very apprehensive our Loss of Prisoners will be very heavy from the Eastward, occasioned by the Publication of the resolves—I have repeatedly ordered them to be collected together in that Quarter & lodged in the Barrack at Rutland, but the Council at Boston, will not permit it, as the Stockades are not finished and I know not when they will be—*I enclose their resolve on this Head*—I can assure you Sir, that the whole delays relative to the Barracks w^h. might have been compleated last November, are entirely owing to the Board of War, to whom I represented this Matter in July last, and could not get heard on the Subject, alledging that the Councill were the best Judges, but I am sorry to say that my predictions are verified in the fullest manner & several Thousand pounds entirely sunk to the Continent.

In Decr. last the Board of War desired me to endeavour to get a rough set of Barracks knocked up in Connecticut; accordingly I ordered an Estimate of them to be made, advising at the same time with Govr Trumbull—It has just been handed to me, but unhappily I am sorry to say it bears to great a Complexion of the Times—It is so extravagant & beyond all bounds, that I enclose it more as a Curiosity than any expectation of carrying it into Execution—Alass Sir can no Stop be put to this universal resolution of destroying the whole Continent—If it cannot I will venture to predict as inevitable destruction to our Cause as if we had the united Forces of the world ag^t us—I am afraid the extent of this secret mischief is not yet fully known *by Congress*. It pervades almost ever Pore of the Body Politick and is beating it to a general dissolution—My deputy in State of N York writes me that he cannot get wheat to send into New York under 20/ p^r Bushell—

I forgot to mention in my last, that when at New York, I was informed by our Officers in General, that a poor Woman in the City, (who had exerted herself beyond all expectations in favour of our unhappy Prisoners, especially in their greatest distress in the winter of 1777, and thereby saved the Lives of many) was now in great distress herself for want of flour, they therefore joined in a Petition, that some handsome recompence might be made her, assuring me that she had spent almost her whole substance in their relief—I therefore ordered her 5 Barrells of flour, which I hope will meet the Approbation of the Board—I also found great difficulties arising from employing the comon Boatmen in transporting the Provisions from Jersey to New York, I therefore purchased a good Boat in Company with the Boatman (a man of good Character) for which we gave £200—Her name is the Sloop Plenty—As I had no orders for so doing, I took the one half in my own name, if the Board is satisfied with the measure, I mean it for the publick Advantage, and will charge the States with the £100—if not I must make the best of it I can—As the Time draws nigh for my leaving my Office, my Year being closed the 12th of Aprill next, there would be great Propriety in the Person who is to succeed me, being with me a few weeks before he takes possession of the office: I could wish to know the Person as soon as possible, especially as my Absence will be necessary, at the meeting of the Com^r. for settling the Cartel—I have lately rec^d a Letter from Mr Franklin my Agent at Philadelphia, informing me that he has Liberty to purchase clothing for our Prisoners, & that he is engaged in that Business—My Deputy in Boston informs me that if permission was given, he could exchange a great number of the Convention Officers—Mr Skene has solicited to be exchanged for the Hon^e. John Fell Esqr—*I enclose you an Acc^t of Mr Pierpoints the State Commissary of Prisoners in Boston, that you may judge*

To Titus Lewis

Sir   Camp V. F. [Valley Forge] March 24th 1778
     Yours of the 12th. Ins^t. came to hand last night and in Consequence of which I have wrote to Providence ordering Mr Furneaux to be sent in to Rhode Island as soon as possible, in Exchange for Capt. Manley late of Hancock, in the mean time have enclosed a Certificate of the same that Capt. Manley may not be unnecessarily detained as you may depend on the Exchange being effected without delay

Am &
P. S. I should be glad to know if the Mermaids men are arrived &
what Prisoners of ours are liberated in Consequence—

Lewis was Commissary of "Sea Prisoners" which included both civilian and naval
personnel who were held captive. These men did not normally fall under
Boudinot's jurisdiction but were handled separately.

To Archibald Campbell

Sir,   Camp V. F. [Valley Forge] March 24th 1778
    My acknowledgements are due for your polite Letter of the 8th.
Inst[t]. Which was delivered to me last evening—
    I am truly concerned that so many unlucky & unforeseen
Accidents should retard your liberation—I can assure you Sir that I
have not been unmindfull of you—I have lately been on a visit to our
Prisoners in New York, where I solicited your Exchange for Coll.
Allen in Person; offering to send the orders Express from that City for
your going immediately into New Port, but was refused more than
once, and I have some reason to believe thro' the intervention of the
disaffected Inhabitants—Gen[l]. Prescott had been arrived several
Weeks, *on the agreem[t]. between our two Generals,* but I could not
obtain Gen[l] Lee's release, because orders had not been sent as was
expected from Gen[l] Howe—On my return to Jersey, I was prohibited
giving orders for your immediate going on Parole into New Port as I
intended on acc[t]. of the detention of Gen[l]. Lee—However to prevent
the inconveniency to you as far as my Power, I wrote to my Deputy,
to forward you on to Morris Town in Jersey where I would meet
you—This Letter will have reached you before this, but if it should
not, I intend by this Opportunity to M[r]. Messereau, ordering him to
give you the proper Passports for coming to Morris Town, where I
have order the Quarter Master to provide you with proper Quarters till
you can write me a Line—I am sensible this will be a disagreeable &
expensive Journey, but I am clear it will be to your advantage on the
whole—notwithstanding if you prefer going into New Port & will
signify it to me, I will do all I can to accomplish the matter—nothing is
wanting but for Gen[l] Howe to say he will send out M[r] Allen for you—
    There has been an Agree[t] lately made between our two Generals
for a mutual Exchange of Prisoners on Parole—on which one General

Officer & 4 or 5 field Officers have been sent in and others are demanded in return, but can get no Answer, tho' many Weeks have been elapsed—Commissioners meet on the 31st. Inst^t. to perfect a general Cartel if possible—This is a desirable Event & hope it will be accomplished—

March 27th. Have rec^d. the three Orders on the Loan Office for thirty three Thousand Dollars, enclosed in Col Pickering's Letter—

To Henry Hugh Fergusson

Sir,   Camp V F [Valley Forge] March 27 1778
      I am much surprized to find by yours of the 22^d. Ins^t. that the Officers from Maryland &c are not arrived as I sent them a Passport for that purpose to Lancaster 1[8] days ago—It must arise from their own delay, unless a difficulty has arose with regard to the payment of the Subsistance money that has been advanced for them, which must be repaid before they can leave Lancaster, but I have not heard a word of it, except in the Case of Capt. Battut, L^{ts}. Wilmot & francis who returned from the white Horse Tavern, to Lancaster on that Acc^t.
      I am informed that L^t. Getting is still greatly indisposed & incapable of returning to New York, wherefore necessity obliges us to submit to his Exchange, not withstanding my desire of putting a stop to Officers fixing on their own Exchanges. I shall therefore agree to L^t. Cameron's release, and enclose his Parole accordingly, expecting Mr Gettings in your next—I should be glad of an Order on the Commissary at New York for the release of such of our officers as as mentioned in the list lately sent you, for such as have arrived at Philadelphia & New York—to which you may add Peter Meddagh for L^t. Stratton & D^r. Fullerton for Dr Wier—As to Coll. Delancey you may depend on his being a full Colonel, as he settled this matter himself when at New York in Presence of M^r. Commissary Loring— Enclosed you have a copy of Genl Burgoynes Cert. relating to Cap. Farmer omitted by mistake in my last, and a Copy of Commissary M^{ac}Cullough's Parole, whose liberation I interested myself in last Spring on his Promise of returning again unless exchanged, but had

never heard of him or the other two included with him, since, except that Mr Loring lately exchanged Capt. Gamble on knowing the Circumstances—

I rec^d the Summons for Major West & will forward it by the first Opportunity—I should be glad of serving M^r. Bedford, but the Person mentioned belongs to the State of Jersey, and while there are several of their Inhabitants in the same Predicament with Mr Bedford & of much longer standing I could not take this Exchange upon me—If M^r. John Fell could be released for him I should have no doubt but Mr Cook would be sent in—

I have this Moment rec^d a Letter from Lancaster informing me that the Officers detention is at their own desire, waiting for some Express they have sent back for something they have forgot—
Mermaid is gone to York &c—

I forgot to mention the Case of Mr Webb, who I am sorry to say has broke his Parole by going into Philadelphia without leave—He had permission to come down to the Lines, where he was to make Application for the Liberty he desired, but instead of this, takes Advantage of the Ignorance of some Magistrate or other Person in the Country without Authority & went into the City w^h out acquainting any Person or Officer w^h his Intention—I am therefore ordered to require M^r. Webbs immediate return—I have enquired after M^r. Cavennaugh, but I cannot find any Person that knows any thing of him only that there is a Person of the Name in Maryland—He can only be a Ci[vilian] & therefore cannot expect to be Exchanged for a Military Person.

To William Nicholls

Sir,   Camp V. F. [Valley Forge] March 27th. 1778
In Answer to yours of the 20th. Inst^t., can assure you that you have been misinformed with regard to my stopping *your Cloaths &* Effects on Acc^t. of your not returning by the Time Appointed—I knew nothing of your Cloaths being stopped, till I was well informed that you had acted very unworthily by secretly transmitting a Letter to a Person in the Country, by which he rec^d Information in what manner to

desert to the Enemy—The Politeness with which you have been treated, rendered this Conduct the more aggravated, and on hearing that my deputy at Reading had prevented your Baggage being sent away, I mentioned that he should still keep it in reading as you was to be ordered to return—I am therefore to desire you will immediately return to your Parole, by which means you will have an Opportunity of clearing up the Charge ag^t. you if in your Power—

Capt. Traverse is already Exchanged, and therefore you can have no Expectations from that Quarter—

Nicholls was Captain of the *Eagle*, a British packet ship.

To Lewis Pintard

D^r. Sir,   Camp V F [Valley Forge] March 28th. 1778
Your favours of the 16th. & 20th. Inst^t. have come safe to hand—I cannot conceive what occasions the delay in sending you the flour—I left a large Quantity at Brunswick—I expected you would receive two or three Boats load from Monmouth, and I have sent Express to Livingston's Mannor for the purchase of 20000 Bush^{ls}. of wheat—I have also engaged 2000 Bush^{ls}. In Jersey—from all these resources think you will most certainly be supplied—I am the more anxious about this matter as I intend to resign the office on the 12th. Aprill, when I must beg you will close the Acc^{ts}. as I shall make a Point of not leaving Jersey till all your Engagements are fully paid—I never knew of Capt. Moore being taken till your Letter came to hand, not suspecting that it was him having left him in New York—I will send immediately for him & forward him either to Philadelphia or New York as well on his Mothers Acc^t as yours—I am so extremely hurried, by my late appointment as one of the Commissioners to settle a Treaty of Genl Exchange, that I cannot attend to any Thing else at present—Have wrote to Jersey to know the meaning of the Delay there with regard to the flour—I send you herewith 16 Dollars for L^t. Lindsey to the Care of Coll Bull—Seven half Jos. & Seven Guineas for Coll Bull—Six half Jos. in a Leather for Coll Megaw—five half Jos. L^t. W^m. M^{ac}Pherson—1 half Jos.—½ Guinea & two Dollars for L^t. Chas. Willson—five half Jos. & one Moidore for Jacob Drew—

To Joshua Mersereau

D^r. Sir,   Camp V. F. [Valley Forge] March 28 1778
    You will justly wonder at my long Silence, indeed I have been so
engaged since my return from New York, that I could not catch Time
enough to embrace any one Opportunity—This in some measure has
been occasioned by a negotiation that is on foot for setting a gen^l
Cartel, in which I am a Commissioner, and we are to meet the 31st.
Ins^t.
    I wrote you some time in February; to forward Coll. Campbell on
to Morris Town, where I will meet him as soon as I know of his
arrival. He writes me that this Letter has not got to hand—If it has
miscarried you will immediately on receipt hereof, obtain the proper
Passports for his coming on to Jersey, and take his Parole accordingly
to remain at Morris Town till farther Orders from the Commander In
Chief or the Com. Gen of Pris.—You will take the advantage of some
General Officer coming this way, who may prevent an Insult being
offered to him on the Journey—The Genl will direct such route as he
thinks proper—Your several Letters from Decr 18 to Feb^{ry}. 25 have
come safe to hand at different Periods—I am perfectly satisfied that
you have done all in your Power to forward Matters for the general
Interest, and I wish I could say so of every Officer in the publick
Service—I am very happy to have the returns of the Prisoners at last,
altho' they fall far short of the numbers I expected had been in those
States—I cannot conceive what has become of all that have been
taken, unless we have been originally imposed upon in the Account of
numbers—I observe what you say in your Several Letters about the
Exchange of the Convention Officers—I would have you encourage it
as much as possible, and if any number of them will apply, I will get
orders to gratify them—keep an Acc^t. of all that make Application and
let me have their Names & rank—If Genl. Burgoyne will give a
Certificate promising that our Officers of equal rank shall be sent out
in Exchange, I should not be averse to your letting the Gent^n. who
applied in your last Letter go with him to Europe or any other inferior
Officers—I should not be fond of field Officers being sent off, without
a particular Order from the General—I doubt not but Genl Redesels
family & Genl Gall may be indulged on their asking it—as Genl.
Thompson was taken in Canada, I think Genl. Burgoyne could release
him—I am astonished & shocked at the frequent Instances I have of

the Extortion of our Eastern Brethern—It is bad enough here, but I think on the whole every thing is at least 50 p^r C^t. cheaper here than with you—It seems to me as if there was a total defection in the Eastern States from their orig^l. purity and I am some times apt to think that our destruction is sure if a Stop cannot be put to the avarice of our pretended Patriots—Iniquity pervades every pore of the Body politick and dissolution is inevitable, if a speedy & violent remedy is not applied—I am of opinion that nothing short of hanging the first man who breaks the late regulations of Prices, will save us—

I know not what to advise you to with regard to purchasing any Thing—I am almost convinced that our State will enforce the regulations at all Events, therefore think you had best delay a little—Send on the Sugar you have at Connecticut as fast as you can—let it stop at Easton or Bask & let me have the [specie] to pay Mr Plum[er] off—

As to the Councill or any other Person (except the General) exchanging Prisoners, you are in the first Place on knowing any Thing of this kind being on foot, to remonstrate ag^t. & expressly forbid it, as contrary to the orders of both Congress and the Commander in Chief—In the next place you are not to discharge any Officer or Solder for any such Purpose, but to inform the officers to be exchanged that their Paroles will still be considered as in force & their Exchange reprobated and in the last Place you are to make a formal report of it to General Heath as a Breech of the Orders you have rec^d.—Indeed this will in some measure be prevented when you get them under your own Care at rutland, as the Councill with then have nothing to do with them—farther than from y^r gen^l superintendency over the whole State—I enclose you the resolves of Congress according to your desire—I have rec^d. the Estimate of the Barracks but am frightened at the amount & therefore shall refer it to Congress—The Extravagance of the Po[rt]ledge [*sic*] Bill you enclosed is beyond all Bounds I shall lay a State of this matter before Congress—I enclose a Draught on the Loan Office in your State for 4000 Dollars, and if you can negotiate this will send you more—You will please to close all your Acc^{ts}. on the 12th. Aprill next, as I intend all shall be fully paid off on that Day, and begin one of a new—Send me the Acc^{ts}. & I will transmit you the Balance—Please to send D^r. Wier in to New Port as soon as possible, as also Capt. Furneaux of the Syren, having agreed for the Exchange of the first for D^r. Fullerton &

the last for Cap Manley—I write to the Govr. of Rhode Island on the same Subject—You will remember that no Officer is ever to be allowed to go in on any Terms or by any Authority without paying off all Arrears—If John D. Whitworth has not been guilty of any thing particularly obnoxious, but is in the predicament of a Prisoner of War only, he ought to be admitted to his Parole—

To William Govat

Sir   March 28th 1778
     Enclosed you have an Acc^t of all the monies I can find that has been paid on Acc^t of the british Pris. by me, or for which I have the Vouchers—You have also an Acc^t. of Henry Haller Esqr deputy Com of Pris. at Reading, which he has sent to me by mistake—I have all the orig^l Vouchers, but think it best not to trust them by this Opportunity—if they are immediately wanted will send them on receiving a Line from you—I wrote you lately desiring you to send me the Bills of Exchange, which I hope got safe to hand—

To Ezekiel Williams

Dr Sir,   Camp V. F. [Valley Forge] March 28 1778
     My long stay at New York and being exceedingly engaged since in the Business of a general Cartel has prevented my writing to you lately—When at New York, I got the Affairs of Prisoners in a much better situation then they have ever yet been—The poor fellows are now well cloathed & well fed and the sick taken proper Care of—I was used with the utmost politeness, and had every Indulgence I could have wished.
     I was greatly surprized to find a number of the Officers from Connecticut in the City, and was very happy to arrive just time enough to prevent the ungenerous Exchange that was going on—I am confident had it taken Place it would have caused a mutiny in the Army—I must beg that you will not suffer a single Officer to leave your department in future by any authority whatever without your Approbation—I am sure the Govr. on the least reflection will see the propriety of it, as the late Practices have so great a Tendency to raise

Jealousies & Animosities, between the Troops of the diff^t. States—This is the reason, the Enemy are so fond of promoting it, by encouraging of these Exchanges—I heard enough of this when in the City—It is generally propagated there, that Govr Trumbull had given out that he would Exchange every Connecticut Officer & Soldier in preference to any other State, and from Appearances, the Southern Officers on Long Island, really believed it, till I convinced them of the absurdity of it—By the resolves of Congress the whole department of Prisoners is vested in me & my deputies—This is from necessity, or the differing Interests of the States, would throw all into Confusion—

I wrote you lately to return Coll. Delancey to New York, if he is not gone in, be very particular in ascertaining his Rank in his Parole, and forward the Paroles or Copies of them to me—

As to Confining the Prisoners, I have long doubted the practicability of it, and have been much surprized at Congress insisting on it, without farther Provision for the purpose—All I can say is that for the present we must do as well as we can according to Circumstances till I can go to Congress, where I hope all matters will be rectified especially when the Genl Cartel is settled—When Prisoners come into your Care, you are not to regard the Paroles which they have given to another deputy, if you think them improper considering the Circumstances of your State, only be carefull that when you alter them, you are to make them close Prisoners till they give you such a one as you desire—I think you ought to lock up Cap Barns without Hesitation You may send Coll. Van Speth & his Lieutenant into New York, on his Parole according to the form sent you lately—Enclosed you have an order on your loan Office for 4000 Dollars, which I hope you can negotiate—Let all your Acc^{ts}. be closed on the 12 Aprill when I will pay them off, and then begin anew—I should be glad you would secure me a Barrell of Salmon in the Season, and a few smoaked or dryed—As to the Officers Board, you are to require of them in Gold or Silver the two Dollars p^r Week you have advanced for them, and the farmers should not ask them more if they are willing to hire as they do, but whatever they agree for besides you have nothing to do with, only you are not to suffer them to receive Continental Money from N York or to break the Laws of your State in selling Gold contrary to your regulations—I am not a little surprized at Capt. Judd & Capt. Flinn being sent in to N York, as our Sea Officers are treated so much worse than those of the Land Service*—I must beg you will apply to the Govr. & get him to remand them both, especially as I have exchanged Capt Manley for Capt Furneaux—I shall enclose you the resolves of Congress for your direction, altho' the late ones ordering a retaliation &c &c with regard to Provisions I do not pretend to execute as a general Exchange is on foot—

*I was not suffered to send on Board of the Prison Ships one rag of Clothing to their relief (tho' I had it all ready made) because it was purchased in New York, with Genl. Howes permission—Every Sea Officer should be confined & not suffered to purchase a rag among us—

I have no objection to the release of John Ireland provided he is altogether a comon Prisoner of War—You may also permit Serj. Maj Green to go in on the Terms you mention, take his Parole accordingly allowing him one Month—I am much surprized & alarmed at M^r. Webbes bringing out such a Sum of money for Capt. Barbine, and think that you ought to rep^t it to the Govr. & take his directions—The rate of Exchange of Hard money is fixed by the Congress Dollar for Dollar, this extends only to what is paid on a publick Acc^t.—L^t. Lundy & the other officers Acc^{ts}. will fall on whoever took him in to New York without seeing them discharged—

To Nicholas Cooke

Sir   Camp V F [Valley Forge] March 28 1778
    Having lately Exchanged Capt. Manley for Cap. Furneaux of the Syren Frigate, I must beg the favour of your giving Orders for his being immediately sent into New Port, which I have engaged shall be done without delay—He must previously pay off all arrears due for his Board &—
    Have the honor &

Cooke was the Governor of Rhode Island.

DOCUMENT CHRONOLOGY

To the Governors and Executive Bodies of the Thirteen States,
    April 17, 1777.
To The Secretary of the Board of War, April 17, 1777.
To Joshua Loring, April 30, 1777.
To Joshua Loring, partial letter, May 5, 1777.
To Lewis Pintard, partial letter.
To Joshua Loring, May 22, 1777.
To Joshua Loring, May 26, 1777.
To Lewis Pintard, May 26, 1777.
To Richard Peters, June 16, 1777.
To the President of the Convention of New York, June 19, 1777.
To Jonathan Trumbull, June 19, 1777.
To the President of the Council of Massachusetts Bay, June 19, 1777.
To David Franks, June 28, 1777.
To Richard Peters, June 30, 1777.
To David Franks, June 30, 1777.
To Robert Richards, June 30, 1777.
To James Mease, June 30, 1777.
To Lewis Pintard, July 1, 1777.
To Robert Magaw, July 1, 1777.
To Robert Lettis Hooper Jr., July 5, 1777.
To James Wilson and Christian Forster, July 5, 1777.
To William Gordon, July 9, 1777.
To The President of the State of Massachusetts Bay, July 9, 1777.
To Jonathan Trumbull, July 9, 1777.
Appointment of John Adam, as Deputy Commissary General of Prisoners,
    July 8, 1777.
Instructions to John Adam, July 9, 1777.
Instructions to Joshua Mersereau, July 9, 1777.
To Lewis Pintard, July 10, 1777.
To Charles Gordon.
To Richard Peters, July 14, 1777.
To Henry Haller, July 22, 1777.
To Richard Peters, July 22, 1777.
To Joseph Barton, July 24, 1777.
To David Franks, July 24, 1777.
To William Livingston, July 26, 1777.

To Lewis Pintard, July 27, 1777.
To William Atlee, August 11, 1777.
To Samuel Miles, August 14, 1777.
To Joshua Mersereau, August 14, 1777.
To John Adam, August 14, 1777.
To Richard Peters, August 15, 1777.
To Lewis Pintard, August 16, 1777.
To Lewis Pintard, August 26, 1777.
To John Campbell, August 27, 1777.
To John Campbell, August 28, 1777.
To Lewis Pintard, September 28, 1777.
To William Howe, September 30, 1777.
To Joshua Loring, October 6, 1777.
To Timothy Pickering, October 19, 1777.
To Lewis Pintard, November 3, 1777.
To Joshua Loring, November 3, 1777.
To The British Commissary of Prisoners, Philadelphia,
    November 12, 1777.
Notations on Letters Sent at Various Times.
To Lewis Pintard, November 13, 1777.
To Robert Lettis Hooper Jr., November 13, 1777.
To John Duyckinck, November 13, 1777.
To Charles Edmonstone, November 13, 1777.
To Abraham B. Bancker, November 13, 1777.
To William Atlee, November 13, 1777.
To Joshua Mersereau November 13, 1777.
To John Adam, November 13, 1777.
To Elbridge Gerry, November 13, 1777.
To Richard Peters, November 13, 1777.
To Joshua Mersereau, November 14, 1777.
To Ezekiel Williams, November 14, 1777.
To Joshua Loring, November 24, 1777.
To Lewis Pintard, November 24, 1777.
To Robert MacKenzie, November 25, 1777.
To William Peterson, December 1, 1777.
To Richard Prescott, December 1, 1777.
To Ezekiel Williams, December 1, 1777.
To Robert Lettis Hooper Jr., December 4, 1777.

To Elisha Lawrence, December 4, 1777.
To Joshua Mersereau, December 14, 1777.
To Robert Lettis Hooper Jr., December 14, 1777.
To Richard Graham, December 22, 1777.
To William Buchanan, December 22, 1777.
To Joseph Holmes, December 23, 1777.
To Thomas Johnson, December 23, 1777.
To George Lindenberger, December 23, 1777.
To Ezekiel Williams, December 23, 1777.
To Robert Haughy, December 28, 1777.
To Thomas Franklin, December 29, 1777.
To Joshua Loring, December 29, 1777.
To James Nielson, December 29, 1777.
To Lewis Pintard, December 29, 1777.
To John Adam, December 30, 1777.
To Joshua Mersereau, December 30, 1777.
To Richard Peters, December 30, 1777, and January 1, 1778.
To Ezekiel Williams, December 30, 1777.
To Henry Hugh Fergusson, December 31, 1777.
To Joseph Holmes, January 2, 1778.
To Robert Haughy, January 3, 1778.
To Jesse Hollingsworth, January 4, 1778.
To Robert Lettis Hooper Jr., January 6, 1778.
To William Atlee, January 7, 1778.
To Thomas Franklin, January 8, 1778.
To Henry Hugh Fergusson, January 8, 1778.
To William Edmestone, January 8, 1778.
To William Govat, January 9, 1778.
To Robert Haughy, January 9, 1778.
To Franciscus Sheffer, January 10, 1778.
To Henry Hugh Fergusson, January 10, 1778.
To Richard Peters, January 11, 1778.
To Jesse or Henry Hollingsworth, January 11, 1778.
To Joshua Mesereau, January 16, 1778.
To Ezekiel Williams, January 16, 1778.
To John Covenhoven, January 17, 1778.
To Robert Dodd, January 17, 1778.
To William Chamberlain, January 19, 1778.

To Joshua Loring, January 19, 1778.
To Henry Clinton, January 20, 1778.
To Lewis Pintard, January 19, 1778.
To Thomas Bradford, January 21, 1778.
To John Adam, January 21, 1778.
To John Campbell, January 23, 1778.
To Lewis Pintard, January 23, 1778.
To Archibald Campbell, January 27, 1778.
To Lewis Pintard, February 9, 1778.
To Robert Livingston, February 21, 1778.
To John Nicoll, February 21, 1778.
To Joshua Mersereau, February 21, 1778.
To John Adam, February 21, 1778.
To Azariah Dunham, February 23, 1778.
To Thomas Peters, March 2, 1778.
To Henry Hugh Fergusson, March 2, 1778.
To William Atlee, March 4, 1778.
Notes on Letter to Patrick Henry, March 7, 1778.
To Henry Haller, March 4, 1778.
To Henry Hugh Fergusson, March 6, 1778.
To Thomas Franklin, March 6, 1778.
To Joshua Loring, March 8, 1778.
To Charles Lee, March 8, 1778.
To Lewis Pintard, March 8, 1778.
To Sylvanus Seely, March 8, 1778.
To Horatio Gates, March 10, 1778.
To William Govat, March 10, 1778.
To Thomas Peters, March 11, 1778.
To William Atlee, March 11, 1778.
To Henry Haller, March 12, 1778.
To George Washington, March 3, 1778.
To Robert Lettis Hooper Jr., March 16, 1778.
To Henry Hugh Fergusson, March 17, 1778.
To John Campbell, March 17, 1778.
To Major Dulley, March 17, 1778.
To William Atlee, March 17, 1778.
To Horatio Gates, March 21, 1778.
To Titus Lewis, March 24, 1778.

To Archibald Campbell, March 24, 1778.
To Henry Hugh Fergusson, March 25, 1778.
To William Nicholls, March 27, 1778.
To Lewis Pintard, March 28, 1778.
To Joshua Mersereau, March 28, 1778.
To William Govat, March 28, 1778.
To Ezekiel Williams, March 28, 1778.
To Nicholas Cooke, March 28, 1778.

FURTHER READINGS ON BOUDINOT AND PRISONERS OF WAR DURING THE AMERICAN REVOLUTION

Alexander, John K. "Forton Prison During the American Revolution: A Case Study of British Prisoner of War Policy and the American Prisoner Response to that Policy." *Essex Institute Historical Collections*, 103 (October 1967), 365-89.

Amerman, Richard H. "Treatment of American Prisoners During the Revolution." *Proceedings of the New Jersey Historical Society*, New Ser., 78 (October 1960), 257-75.

Anderson, Olive. "The Treatment of Prisoners of War in Britain During the American War of Independence." *Bulletin of the Institute of Historical Research*, 28 (May 1955), 63-83.

Becker, Laura L. "Prisoners of War in the American Revolution: A Community Perspective." *Military Affairs*, 46 (December 1982), 169-73.

Beroth, Janet. "The Convention of Saratoga." *Quarterly Journal of the New York State Historical Association*, 8 (July 1927), 257-80.

Boudinot, Elias. "American Prisoners of War in New York: A Report by Elias Boudinot." Ed. David L. Sterling. *William and Mary Quarterly*, 3d Ser., 13 (July 1956), 376-93.

_____. *Journal or Historical Recollections of American Events During the Revolutionary War*. Philadelphia: Frederick Bourquin, 1894.

_____. "Colonel Elias Boudinot's Notes of Two Conferences Held by the American and British Commissioners to Settle a General Cartel for the Exchange of Prisoners of War, 1778." *Pennsylvania Magazine of History and Biography*, 24 (1900), 291-305.

_____. "Colonel Elias Boudinot in New York City, February, 1778." Ed. Helen Jordan. *Pennsylvania Magazine of History and Biography*, 24 (1900), 453-66.

J. J. Boudinot. *The Life Public Service, Addresses and Letters of Elias Boudinot, LL. D.* Boston: Houghton, Mifflin, 1896.

Bowie, Lucy Leigh. The Ancient Barracks at Fredericktown Where Hessian Prisoners Were Quartered During the Revolutionary War. Frederick: Maryland State School for the Deaf, 1939.

_____. "German Prisoners in the American Revolution." *Maryland Historical Magazine*, 40 (September 1945), 185-200.

Bowman, Larry G. *Captive Americans: Prisoners during the American Revolution.* Athens: Ohio University Press, 1977.

_____. "The Pennsylvania Prisoner Exchange Conferences, 1778." *Pennsylvania History,* 45 (July 1978), 257-69.

_____. "Military Parolees on Long Island, 1777-1782." *Journal of Long Island History,* 18 (Spring 1982), 21-29.

Boyd, George A. *Elias Boudinot: Patriot and Statesman, 1740-1821.* Princeton: Princeton University Press, 1952.

Clark, Barbara Louise. E. B.: *The Story of Elias Boudinot IV, his family, his Friends, and his Country.* Philadelphia: Dorrance, 1977.

Clark, Jane, ed. "The Convention Troops and the Perfidy of Sir William Howe." *American Historical Review,* 37 (July 1932), 721-23.

Coffin, Alexander. *The American Captives at New York During the Revolutionary War.* New York: 1865.

Cohen, Sheldon S. "Thomas Wren: Ministering Angel of Forton Prison." *Pennsylvania Magazine of History and Biography,* 103 (July 1979), 279-301.

Dabney, William M. *After Saratoga: The Story of the Convention Army.* Albuquerque: University of New Mexico Press, 1954.

Dandridge, Danske. *American Prisoners of the Revolution.* Charlottesville: Michie, 1911.

Denn, Robert J. "Prison Narratives of the American Revolution." Ph.D. Dissertation, Michigan State University, 1980.

_____. "Captivity Narratives of the American Revolution." *Journal of American Culture,* 2 (Winter 1980), pp. 575-82.

Dixon, Martha W. "Divided Authority: The American Management of Prisoners in the Revolutionary War, 1775-1783." Ph.D. Dissertation, University of Utah, 1977.

Egleston, N. H. "The Newgate of Connecticut: The Simsbury Copper Mines." *Magazine of American History,* 13 (April 1885), 321-34.

Ford, W. C., ed. "British and American Prisoners of War, 1778." *Pennsylvania Magazine of History and Biography,* 17 (1893), 159-74, 316-24.

Hyde, West, and John Andre. "Exchange of Prisoners, 1779." *Historical Magazine,* 8 (June 1864), 200-207.

Knepper, George W. "The Convention Army, 1777-1783." Ph.D. Dissertation, University of Michigan, 1954.

Knight, Betsy. "Prisoner Exchange and Parole in the American Revolution." *William and Mary Quarterly*, 3d Ser., 48 (April 1991), 201-22.

Lewis, George G., and John Mewha. *History of Prisoner of War Utilization by the United States Army, 1776-1945*. Washington: Department of the Army, 1955.

Lingley, Charles R. "The Treatment of Burgoyne's Troops Under the Saratoga Convention." *Political Science Quarterly*, 22 (September 1907), 440-59.

Metzger, Charles H. *The Prisoner in the American Revolution*. Chicago: Loyola University Press, 1971.

Overton, Albert G., and J. W. W. Loose. "An Unusual Discovery: Prisoner-of-War Barracks in Lancaster Used during the Revolutionary War." *Lancaster County Historical Society Journal*, 84 (Trinity 1980), 131-34.

Parsons, John C.. *Letters and Documents of Ezekiel Williams of Wethersfield, Connecticut, Deputy Commissary General of Prisoners within the State of Connecticut* Connecticut: The Acorn Club, 1976.

"Partial List of Officers and Privates of the Continental Army Confined in the Walnut Street Jail, January-May, 1778." *Pennsylvania Magazine of History and Biography*, 42 (1918), 173-74.

Prelinger, Catherine M. "Benjamin Franklin and the American Prisoners of War in England During the American Revolution." *William and Mary Quarterly*, 3d Ser., 32 (April 1975), 261-92.

Richards, Henry Melchoir Muhlenberg. *The Pennsylvania-German in the British Military Prisons of the Revolutionary War*. Lancaster: Pennsylvania-German Society, 1924.

Roddis, Louis H. "The New York Prison Ships in the American Revolution." *U.S. Naval Institute Proceedings* 61 (March 1935), 331-36.

Schieffelin, Jacob. "A British Prisoner of War in the American Revolution: The Experiences of Jacob Schieffelin from Vincennes to Williamsburg, 1779-1780." Edited by Gerald O. Haffner. *Virginia Magazine of History and Biography*, 86 (January 1978), 17-25.

Sparks, Jared, et al. "Report on Exchange of Prisoners during the American Revolution." *Massachusetts Historical Society Proceedings*, 5 (December 1861), 325-47.

Stevens, Mary K. "The Convention Troops in Connecticut." *Connecticut Quarterly*, 3 (April-June 1897), 144-49.

Tanner, Douglas W., Ed. "The Story of the Convention Army." *Albemarle County History*, 41 (1983).

Wall, Alexander J. "The Story of the Convention Army, 1777-1783." *New-York Historical Society Quarterly Bulletin*, 11 (October 1927), 67-97.

West, Charles E. "Prison Ships in the American Revolution." *Journal of American History*, 5 (January 1911), 121-28.

White, Herbert H. "British Prisoners of War in Hartford During the Revolution." *Connecticut Historical Society Bulletin*, 19 (July 1954), 65-81.

INDEX

101, 104, 116, 117, 125; letters to,
92, 121
Campbell, Ensign, 41
Campbell, John, 40; letters to, 34,
35, 91, 116
Campbell, Robert, 36
Campbell, Thomas, 36, 67
Canada, 21, 40, 64
Carlisle, John, 43
Carlisle, Pa., prisoners at, 96
Carmichael, Robert, 107, 115, 118
Cattle, 64, 67, 70, 72, 78, 79, 86, 90,
92, 95, 99, 113
Cavenaugh, Mr., 115
Cavennaugh, Mr., 99, 123
Centuacy, Baron de, 41
Chamberlain, William, letter to, 86
Chandler, Mr., 32
Charlton, John, 59
Chesapeake Bay, 27
Chesley, James, 43
Chester County, Pa., 58
Chickley, Samuel, 32
Church, Dr., 51
Clarkson, Jere., 40
Clinton, George, 67
Clinton, Henry, 88, 106
Clothing, 14, 20, 21, 32, 39, 52, 53,
66, 69, 71, 112, 120; shortages of,
23, 36, 37, 40, 41, 69, 73, 78, 82,
111; cost of, 93
Clymer, Daniel, 28, 64, 73, 99, 113
Cochran, Mr., 52
Coffee, 20
Collins, Captain, 94
Collins, Mr., 86
Combs, Martin, 40
Combs, Stephen, 40
Commissary of Prisoners in the
British Army; letter to, 41
Connecticut; barracks for prisoners
in, 11; prisoners in, 17, 20, 37,
41, 51, 54, 62, 65, 70, 84
Connecticut River; prisoner barracks
to be constructed on, 68
Connolly/Conolly, Mr., 96, 105

Continental Congress, 2, 9, 11, 12,
13, 19, 33, 39, 44, 47, 48, 51, 56,
58, 65, 67, 71, 76, 84, 85, 86, 99,
104, 105, 108, 118, 119, 128
Cook, Mr., 123
Corn, 39, 63, 75
Courtland, Major, 35
Covenhoven, John, letter to, 85
Crawford, John, 32
Crawford, William, 32
Crewe, Richard, 98
Custis, Thomas, 53

D

Darby, Nathaniel, 53
Davis, James, 98
Davis, Rezin, 90
Dean, Mr., 46
Deane, Mr., 50
Delancey, Oliver, 67, 122, 128
Delaware River, 63, 64, 65, 72, 74,
81, 82; American defense of, 49,
50, 51;
enemy ships captured on, 78, 85
Dodd, Robert, 87; letter to, 86
Dongan, Colonel, 91
Donop, Carl Emil Kurt von, 49, 50
Drew, Jacob, 124
Drew, Louis, 78
Drummer, Nesbit, 33
Dulley, Major, 117
Dumfries, Va., Hessian prisoners at,
40, 41
Dungan, Colonel, 35, 40
Dunham, Azariah, letter to, 95
Dunham, James, 99
Dunham, Samuel, 99
Duyckinck, John, 43, 58; letter to, 44

E

Easton, Pa., 44, 56, 59; English
prisoners at, 44; prisoners at, 15,
27, 40, 43, 55, 76, 77
Edie, John, 40
Edmestone, William, letter to, 79

Edmondstone/Edmeston, Major, 115
Edmonstone, Charles, 40, 43; letters
  to, 44
Elizabethtown, N.J., 38, 89, 90, 102,
  103

F

Falls, Mr., 98
Farmer, Captain, 122
Fell, John, 4, 7, 8, 10, 34, 36, 120,
  123
Fenwick, George, 107
Ferguson, William, 33
Fergusson, Elizabeth, 32
Fergusson, Henry Hugh, 63, 64, 70,
  88, 99, 105, 111; letters to, 72,
  78, 81, 96, 98, 114, 122
Finney, Walter, 90
Flahavan, John, 32, 88
Flemington, N.J., 87
Flinn/Flynn, Charles, 128
Flour, 22, 25, 26, 31, 38, 42, 51, 52,
  60, 63-66, 70, 71, 72, 74, 75-79,
  81, 82, 85-87, 89, 91, 92, 99, 100,
  102, 113
Folkerson, Phil., 20, 21
Food rations for prisoners, 55, 56,
  57, 74, 112, 114
Forster, Christian, 25, 28, 47, 48;
  letter to, 15
Fort Frederick, Md., 61, 105
Fort Mercer, N.J., attack on, 49, 50,
  52, 73
Fort Mifflin, Pa., American defense
  of, 50
Foster, Lieutenant, 115
France, 47; no news from, 30
Francis, Captain, 84, 122
Francis, Lieutenant, 107, 118
Francis, S., 5
Frank, Thomas, 75
Franklin, Thomas, 60, 72, 75, 79,
  90, 108, 111, 112, 113, 120;
  letters to, 63, 78, 99
Franklin, William, 105

Franks, David, 6, 7, 23, 31, 36, 41,
  55, 59, 61; letters to, 11, 13, 25
Fulkerson, Philip, 33
Fullerton, Edward, 90, 115, 122, 126
Furneaux, Tobias, 120, 126, 129

G

Galbreath, Major, 98
Gale, John, 43
Gall, W. R. von, 125
Gamble, Thomas, 8, 41, 87, 123
Gates, Horatio, 48; letters to, 103,
  118
Germantown, Battle of, 49
Gerry, Elbridge, letter to, 47
Gettig/Getting, Christopher, 114
Getting, Lieutenant, 122
Gibbons, John, 5
Gilchrist, George, 53
Glasgow Forge, Pa., 83
Goodrich, Captain, 97
Goodwin, Captain, 64
Gordon, Charles, letter to, 21
Gordon, William, 20; letter to, 16
Goshen, N.Y., prisoners at, 47
Govat, William, letters to, 79, 105,
  127
Governors of the Thirteen States,
  letter to, 2
Graham, Mr., 61
Graham, Richard, letter to, 59
Green, Ebenezer, 40
Green, John, 40
Green, Sergeant-Major, 129
Greene, Christopher, 4
Grover, Thomas, 40

H

Hager, Jonathan, 21
Hale, Daniel, 91
Hall, Elihu, 52
Haller, Henry, 28, 43, 79, 97, 127;
  letters to, 23, 98, 107
Haller, William, 42

www.ingramcontent.com/pod-product-compliance
Lightning Source LLC
Chambersburg PA
CBHW060348090426
42734CB00011B/2069